# Table of Contents

Introduction to CryptoGuide .................................................................. 4

Chapter- 1: A comprehensive guide featuring 100 commonly asked questions regarding Cryptocurrency and associated terminology, accompanied by thorough explanations and straightforward answers: ........................... 8

Chapter- 2: 25 main legal and 25 main illegal aspects of Cryptocurrency as of 2024, explained in a simple language: ................................................ 38

    Legal Aspects ................................................................................. 38

    Illegal Aspects ................................................................................ 41

Chapter- 3: 50 points on "Why it is safe to invest in Cryptocurrency" and 50 points on "Why it is unsafe to invest in Cryptocurrency" in easy and simple way. ................................................................................................ 45

    The following 50 points outline the reasons why investing in Cryptocurrency can be considered safe: ............................................ 45

    The following 50 points outline the reasons why investing in Cryptocurrency can be considered unsafe: ........................................ 53

Chapter- 4: The following guidelines are designed to assist individuals in making responsible and informed decisions regarding Cryptocurrency investments, enabling them to effectively navigate the complexities of the market while managing associated risks. ................................................ 61

    50 Points- You should be always aware of before investing for Cryptocurrency ................................................................................ 61

    50 Points- Before investment never forget to what you have to do or not to do and don't make haste to invest for Cryptocurrency ............................. 68

Chapter- 5: 50 Safest Ways to Invest in Cryptocurrency ........................ 75

Chapter- 6: Some of the major markets and platforms where you can invest in Cryptocurrencies: ............................................................................. 83

Chapter- 7: Although no investment is completely devoid of risk, certain cryptocurrencies are typically regarded as safer options due to their well-established reputations, significant market presence, and robust development teams. Below is a compilation of 25 widely recognized cryptocurrencies that are frequently perceived as relatively safer investments, accompanied by reasons for their stability. ........................................... 88

Chapter- 8: Investing in Cryptocurrency can be exciting and potentially profitable, but it comes with several risks. Here's a breakdown of the main risk factors involved, explained in simple and human-friendly terms: ............ 94

Chapter- 9: Investing in Cryptocurrency is open to a broad range of individuals and entities, but there are some important considerations and requirements based on personal circumstances and regulatory environments. Here's a detailed look at "Who can invest in Cryptocurrency": ................... 100

Chapter- 10: Full form and definition of each abbreviation used in the Cryptocurrency space: ................................................................................ 104

    General Terms ..................................................................................... 104

    Technical Terms.. ................................................................................. 105

    Cryptocurrency Exchanges and Wallets ............................................ 109

    Investment and Financial Terms ........................................................ 110

    Security Terms ..................................................................................... 110

    Blockchain Terms ................................................................................ 111

    Miscellaneous Terms .......................................................................... 112

Chapter- 11: Some important "A to Z" simplified, point-by-point explanation of Cryptocurrency: ..................................................................................... 113

# Introduction to CryptoGuide

We are pleased to introduce CryptoGuide, your all-encompassing and accessible resource for everything related to Cryptocurrency. Whether you are a novice or seeking to enhance your understanding, this book aims to navigate you through the often perplexing and intricate realm of digital currencies in a clear and concise manner.

CryptoGuide encompasses a broad spectrum of subjects, ensuring you establish a robust foundation for making informed choices. Below is an overview of the content you will discover within:

## 1. 100 Commonly Asked Questions About Cryptocurrency and Related Terminology

This section elucidates the most frequently posed inquiries regarding Cryptocurrency, offering comprehensive explanations in straightforward language. Whether you wish to learn about the workings of Bitcoin, the fundamentals of blockchain technology, or the secure storage of your digital assets, we have you covered.

## 2. 25 Legal and 25 Illegal Aspects of Cryptocurrency as of 2024

As the Cryptocurrency landscape continues to develop, so too do the associated laws and regulations. In this section, we clarify the essential legal and illegal facets you should be aware of, empowering you to navigate the regulatory landscape with confidence and legality.

## 3. 50 Reasons Supporting the Safety of Cryptocurrency Investment and 50 Reasons Highlighting Its Risks

Investing in Cryptocurrency can evoke both excitement and apprehension. Here, we present 50 arguments in favor of the safety of Cryptocurrency investments, alongside 50 points that outline the potential risks. Our objective is to furnish a balanced perspective, enabling you to evaluate the advantages and disadvantages before making investment choices.

## 4. Guidelines for Cryptocurrency Investing: The Do's and Don'ts

To assist you in making prudent investment decisions, we have curated a list of do's and don'ts. These practical recommendations are intended to steer you through the complexities of the Cryptocurrency market, ensuring that you make informed choices while effectively managing risks.

## 5. 50 Secure Approaches to Investing in Cryptocurrency

Safety remains a paramount concern for investors. In this section, we present 50 strategies and techniques designed to facilitate secure investments in Cryptocurrency, aiming to reduce potential risks while enhancing your likelihood of success.

## 6. Key Markets and Platforms for Cryptocurrency Investment

Understanding where to invest is equally crucial as knowing the methods of investment. We offer an overview of the primary markets and platforms available for buying, selling, and trading cryptocurrencies, assisting you in identifying the optimal starting points for your investment endeavors.

## 7. 25 Notable and Relatively Safer Cryptocurrencies to Explore

Although no investment is devoid of risk, certain cryptocurrencies are generally perceived as safer due to their robust market presence and dedicated development teams. We introduce you to 25 such cryptocurrencies, detailing the reasons they are regarded as more stable options for your investment portfolio.

## 8. Grasping the Risks Associated with Cryptocurrency Investment

Investing in Cryptocurrency entails a unique set of risks. This section delineates the principal risk factors involved, presenting them in straightforward and relatable terms. By comprehending these risks, you will be better equipped to navigate the unpredictable landscape of digital assets.

## 9. Who is Eligible to Invest in Cryptocurrency?

Cryptocurrency investment is open to a diverse array of individuals; however, significant considerations arise based on personal circumstances and local regulations. In this section, we examine who can engage in Cryptocurrency investment, along with the essential factors to contemplate before embarking on this journey.

## 10. Comprehensive Guide to Cryptocurrency Abbreviations, Full Form and their Definitions

The Cryptocurrency domain is replete with terminology and abbreviations that can often be perplexing. We have assembled an extensive list of these terms, offering clear definitions to aid in your understanding of the Cryptocurrency lexicon.

## 11. Comprehensive Overview of "A to Z" Cryptocurrency: Simplified Insights

In this concluding section, we present a detailed, alphabetical breakdown of Cryptocurrency, facilitating a clearer understanding of its essential principles and keeping you well-informed. CryptoGuide serves as your primary reference for all aspects of Cryptocurrency, delivering practical guidance and straightforward explanations. Whether you are a first-time investor or seeking to broaden your understanding, this book equips you with the knowledge necessary to make informed and assured choices in the realm of digital assets. Welcome to your exploration of Cryptocurrency—let us embark on this journey together!

# 100 Frequently Asked Questions

Chapter- 1: A comprehensive guide featuring 100 commonly asked questions regarding Cryptocurrency and associated terminology, accompanied by thorough explanations and straightforward answers:

### 1. Question- What is meant by Cryptocurrency?
**Answer-** Cryptocurrency refers to a digital or virtual currency that employs cryptographic techniques for security purposes. Unlike conventional currencies, cryptocurrencies are decentralized and function on a technology known as blockchain, which serves as a distributed ledger maintained by a network of computers, referred to as nodes. This decentralized characteristic removes the necessity for intermediaries such as banks, facilitating direct transactions between users. Cryptocurrencies can serve multiple functions, including online shopping, investment opportunities, and as a method for transferring value internationally.

### 2. Question- How does Cryptocurrency work?
**Answer-** Cryptocurrency function is a operation of cryptocurrencies is based on blockchain technology. A blockchain consists of a series of blocks, each containing a compilation of transactions. When a new transaction takes place, it is aggregated with other transactions into a block. This block is subsequently appended to the blockchain through a consensus mechanism, which verifies and confirms the legitimacy of the transactions.

The process is safeguarded by cryptographic methods, making it challenging to modify previous transactions. Nodes within the network preserve copies of the blockchain, thereby ensuring both transparency and security.

**3. Question- What is meant by Blockchain technology?**
**Answer-** Blockchain technology is characterized by a decentralized ledger system where information is organized in blocks that are sequentially linked to form a chain. Each block encompasses a collection of transactions and a reference to the preceding block, establishing a chronological sequence. This configuration guarantees that once information is recorded, it cannot be easily altered or erased. Blockchain operates on a distributed network of computers (nodes), with each node holding a copy of the blockchain. Consensus mechanisms, such as Proof of Work or Proof of Stake, are employed to validate and reach agreement on transactions, thereby ensuring the integrity and security of the blockchain.

**4. Question- What is meant by Bitcoin?**
**Answer-** Bitcoin is recognized as the pioneering and most prominent Cryptocurrency, established in 2009 by an unidentified individual or group known as Satoshi Nakamoto. It functions on a decentralized blockchain and is frequently likened to digital gold due to its finite supply and role as a store of value. Bitcoin employs a Proof of Work consensus mechanism, wherein miners engage in solving intricate mathematical challenges to authenticate transactions and incorporate them into the blockchain. Transactions involving Bitcoin are documented in a public ledger, and the network operates independently of a central authority, facilitating a peer-to-peer system for value transfer.

**5. Question- What is meant by Ethereum?**
**Answer-** Ethereum is a blockchain platform that transcends mere Cryptocurrency, enabling the development of decentralized applications (dApps) and smart contracts. Introduced in 2015 by

Vitalik Buterin and a team of collaborators, Ethereum offers a programmable blockchain that allows developers to construct their own decentralized applications utilizing smart contracts. These smart contracts are self-executing agreements with their conditions encoded directly into the software, facilitating automated and trustless transactions. Ether (ETH) serves as the native Cryptocurrency of the Ethereum network, utilized for transaction fees and computational services.

## 6. Question- What is meant by Smart Contract?

**Answer-** A smart contract is defined as a self-executing agreement with its stipulations encoded on the blockchain. It autonomously enforces and executes the terms of the contract when specific conditions are satisfied, eliminating the necessity for intermediaries. Smart contracts operate on blockchain platforms such as Ethereum, fostering trustless interactions among parties. For instance, a smart contract could be programmed to automatically release payment upon the completion of a service, thereby minimizing the potential for fraud and enhancing operational efficiency.

## 7. Question- What is meant by Cryptocurrency Wallet?

**Answer-** A Cryptocurrency wallet is a digital instrument that enables individuals to store, transmit, and receive cryptocurrencies. It comprises a pair of cryptographic keys: a public key, which serves as an address for receiving funds, and a private key, which is utilized to authorize transactions and access the stored assets. Wallets can be categorized as software-based, such as applications or online platforms, or hardware-based, which are physical devices that keep keys offline. The level of security associated with a wallet is contingent upon the protection of the private key, as possession of this key grants control over the corresponding funds.

**8. Question- What is meant by Public Key?**
**Answer-** A public key is a cryptographic identifier that facilitates the reception of Cryptocurrency. It is generated from the private key and is shared with others to enable the receipt of funds. The public key works in tandem with the private key to establish a unique address on the blockchain, which can be utilized for receiving Cryptocurrency transactions. In contrast, the private key is essential for signing and authorizing transactions originating from that address.

**9. Question- What is meant by Private Key?**
**Answer-** A private key is a confidential cryptographic identifier that grants access to and control over Cryptocurrency held within a wallet. It plays a vital role in the security framework, enabling the owner to sign transactions and validate ownership of the associated funds. It is imperative to maintain the confidentiality and security of private keys, as unauthorized access can lead to the theft of Cryptocurrency. Typically, private keys are stored securely, either in a hardware wallet or within an encrypted software wallet.

**10. Question- What is meant by Cryptocurrency Exchange?**
**Answer-** A Cryptocurrency exchange is a digital platform that facilitates the buying, selling, and trading of cryptocurrencies. These exchanges can be categorized as either centralized or decentralized. Centralized exchanges are managed by a company and provide various functionalities, including trading pairs, integration with fiat currencies, and customer support services. In contrast, decentralized exchanges (DEXs) function without a central governing body, enabling users to engage in peer-to-peer trading directly on the blockchain. Typically, exchanges impose transaction fees and may offer supplementary services such as staking or lending.

## 11. Question- What is meant by Decentralized Exchange (DEX)?

**Answer-** A decentralized exchange (DEX) refers to a specific kind of Cryptocurrency exchange that operates independently of a central authority. Rather than depending on a single organization or server, DEXs utilize smart contracts to enable direct trades between users. This structure enhances privacy and security, as users maintain control over their assets and conduct transactions directly from their wallets. Additionally, DEXs mitigate the risk of hacking since they do not store significant amounts of user funds in a centralized repository. Notable examples of DEXs include Uniswap and SushiSwap.

## 12. Question- What is meant by Centralized Exchange?

**Answer-** A centralized exchange is a platform that is managed by a company, serving as an intermediary for Cryptocurrency transactions between buyers and sellers. Users are required to create accounts on the exchange and deposit their assets into the exchange's wallet. The platform is responsible for matching orders, executing trades, and safeguarding user funds. Centralized exchanges often offer extra features such as customer support, fiat currency integration, and sophisticated trading tools. However, users must place their trust in the exchange regarding the security of their funds and personal data. Prominent examples include Coinbase, Binance, and Kraken.

## 13. Question- What is meant by Token?

**Answer-** A token is defined as a digital asset that is created and governed on an established blockchain, such as Ethereum. Tokens can embody various forms of assets or utilities, including ownership stakes in a project (security tokens), access rights to a platform (utility tokens), or even tangible assets (asset-backed tokens). In contrast to coins, which function on their own blockchains, tokens are generated through smart contracts and are frequently utilized within particular ecosystems or platforms. They can be exchanged, employed for transactions, or grant access to specific features within a blockchain initiative.

## 14. Question- What is meant by Coin?
**Answer-** A coin refers to a category of Cryptocurrency that functions on its own dedicated blockchain. Notable examples include Bitcoin (BTC), which operates on the Bitcoin blockchain, and Ether (ETH), which is based on the Ethereum blockchain. Coins are primarily utilized as a medium of exchange, a store of value, and a unit of account, facilitating the transfer of value. They can be mined, traded, and utilized for transactions within their respective networks.

## 15. Question- What is meant by Mining?
**Answer-** Mining is the procedure through which new Cryptocurrency transactions are authenticated and incorporated into the blockchain. This process entails solving intricate mathematical problems using specialized computing equipment. In proof-of-work (PoW) blockchains, such as Bitcoin, miners vie to resolve these challenges, and the first to succeed is permitted to append a new block to the blockchain, receiving Cryptocurrency as a reward. Mining plays a crucial role in maintaining the security and integrity of the blockchain by making it computationally challenging to modify previous transactions.

## 16. Question- What is meant by Hash Function?
**Answer-** A hash function is a mathematical procedure that takes an input, often referred to as a "message," and generates a fixed-size string of bytes, commonly known as a hash value. In the realm of Cryptocurrency, hash functions play a crucial role in creating unique identifiers for both blocks and transactions. For instance, Bitcoin utilizes the SHA-256 hash function to generate a 64-character hash for each block. These functions are essential for maintaining data integrity, as they produce a distinct hash for every input, facilitating the detection of any alterations made to the data.

**17. Question- What is meant by Proof of Work (PoW)?**
**Answer-** Proof of Work (PoW) is a consensus protocol employed by certain cryptocurrencies, such as Bitcoin, to authenticate and incorporate transactions into the blockchain. In this system, miners engage in competition to resolve intricate mathematical challenges. The miner who successfully solves the problem first is granted the opportunity to append a new block of transactions to the blockchain and receives a reward in the form of Cryptocurrency. PoW demands substantial computational resources and energy, rendering it secure yet resource-intensive.

**18. Question- What is meant by Proof of Stake (PoS)?**
**Answer-** Proof of Stake (PoS) is a consensus mechanism in which validators are selected to generate new blocks and confirm transactions based on the quantity of coins they possess and are prepared to "stake" as collateral. In contrast to PoW, which depends on computational capabilities, PoS is determined by the volume of Cryptocurrency held. Validators are motivated to behave honestly due to their financial investment in the network. PoS is regarded as a more energy-efficient alternative to PoW.

**19. Question- What is meant by Hard Fork?**
**Answer-** A hard fork refers to a substantial and incompatible modification of a blockchain's protocol, leading to the establishment of a new blockchain that diverges from the original. Such forks arise from disagreements within the community or among developers regarding the project's future direction. Consequently, a hard fork results in two distinct blockchains, each governed by its own set of rules and associated Cryptocurrency. A notable instance of a hard fork is the division between Bitcoin and Bitcoin Cash.

**20. Question- What is meant by Soft Fork?**
**Answer-** A soft fork is characterized as a change to a blockchain's protocol that remains backward-compatible. In contrast to a hard

fork, a soft fork does not generate a new blockchain; rather, it implements updates that align with the existing rules. Nodes that have not adopted the new protocol can still validate transactions, although they may lack the ability to fully engage with the new features. Soft forks are typically employed to facilitate gradual enhancements and modifications to the blockchain.

## 21. Question- What is meant by Cryptocurrency Address?

**Answer-** A Cryptocurrency address is defined as a distinct sequence of characters that signifies a destination for Cryptocurrency transactions. This address is generated from the public key and serves as an account number for users to receive funds. Typically alphanumeric, addresses are unique to each Cryptocurrency. For instance, a Bitcoin address generally begins with a "1" or "3," whereas an Ethereum address starts with "0x."

## 22. Question- What is meant by Ledger?

**Answer-** A ledger serves as a systematic record-keeping mechanism that monitors and documents transactions. In the realm of Cryptocurrency, a ledger is synonymous with a blockchain, which functions as a decentralized and unchangeable record of all transactions executed within the network. Each block within the blockchain encompasses a collection of transactions, and the blockchain ledger guarantees that these transactions are transparent, secure, and immutable once they have been confirmed.

## 23. Question- What is meant by Node?

**Answer-** A node refers to a computer that engages in the blockchain network by preserving a copy of the blockchain and verifying transactions. Nodes interact with one another to maintain the accuracy and uniformity of the blockchain. Various types of nodes exist, including full nodes that retain the complete blockchain and lightweight nodes that only keep a portion of the blockchain data.

## 24. Question- What is meant by Cryptocurrency Wallet?

**Answer-** A Cryptocurrency wallet is a digital instrument designed to store your private and public keys, enabling you to send and receive Cryptocurrency. It can take the form of software (such as desktop, mobile, or web wallets) or hardware (physical devices that securely store keys offline). Wallets play a crucial role in managing your Cryptocurrency assets, and the degree of security is contingent upon the wallet type and the measures taken to safeguard your private keys.

## 25. Question- What is meant by Cryptocurrency Transaction?

**Answer-** A Cryptocurrency transaction refers to the process of transferring Cryptocurrency from one digital address to another. These transactions are documented on the blockchain and include essential information such as the sender's address, the recipient's address, the amount being transferred, and a digital signature that serves to authenticate the transaction. Once a transaction is incorporated into a block and validated by the network, it becomes a permanent part of the immutable ledger.

## 26. Question- What is meant by a Block in a Blockchain?

**Answer-** A block within a blockchain serves as a storage unit that contains a collection of transactions. Each block comprises a list of transactions, a timestamp indicating when the block was created, a reference to the preceding block via a hash, and a distinct identifier (hash) for the block itself. The interconnection of blocks forms a chain, establishing a secure and chronological record of all transactions recorded on the blockchain.

## 27. Question- What is meant by Consensus Mechanism?

**Answer-** A consensus mechanism is a set of rules employed by blockchain networks to establish agreement on the legitimacy of transactions and the overall state of the blockchain. This mechanism guarantees that all nodes within the network come to a unified understanding regarding the status of the ledger. Notable consensus mechanisms include Proof of Work (PoW), Proof of Stake (PoS), and Delegated Proof of Stake (DPoS), each utilizing its unique approach to achieve consensus.

## 28. Question- What is meant by Smart Contract?

**Answer-** A smart contract is an automated agreement that executes itself based on pre-defined conditions encoded within its programming. It autonomously enforces and carries out the stipulations of the contract once the specified criteria are satisfied. Smart contracts operate on blockchain networks, such as Ethereum, and remove the necessity for intermediaries by facilitating transactions and enforcing agreements in a trustless environment.

## 29. Question- What is meant by Token Sale?

**Answer-** A token sale refers to a fundraising initiative in which a nascent Cryptocurrency project offers its tokens to initial investors. These sales can manifest in various formats, including Initial Coin Offerings (ICOs), Initial Exchange Offerings (IEOs), and Security Token Offerings (STOs). Participants acquire tokens with the expectation that their value will appreciate as the project progresses. Token sales serve to generate capital for the initiative and frequently grant early access to the project's functionalities or services.

## 30. Question- What is meant by Decentralized Application (dApp)?

**Answer-** A decentralized application (dApp) is a software application that functions on a decentralized network, such as a blockchain. In contrast to conventional applications that rely on centralized servers, dApps utilize smart contracts to perform their operations and engage with the blockchain. This decentralized model enhances security, transparency, and resistance to censorship. Notable examples of dApps include decentralized finance (DeFi) platforms and decentralized exchanges (DEXs).

## 31. Question- What is meant by a Fork?

**Answer-** A fork is defined as a modification or update to the protocol of a blockchain. There are primarily two categories: soft forks and hard forks. A soft fork is an update that remains compatible with previous versions, meaning not all nodes are required to upgrade. Conversely, a hard fork results in the creation of a new, incompatible version of the blockchain, leading to the existence of two distinct blockchains. Forks may arise from disagreements among developers or as a means to introduce new features and enhancements.

## 32. Question- What is meant by Cryptocurrency Mining Pool?

**Answer-** A mining pool is an assembly of Cryptocurrency miners who collaborate by merging their computational power to enhance their likelihood of successfully mining a block. By consolidating their resources, miners can achieve block solutions more frequently and receive a portion of the block reward that corresponds to their individual contributions. Mining pools serve to minimize the fluctuations in mining rewards, thereby offering more stable payouts to their members.

## 33. Question- What is meant by a Hard Cap in an ICO?

**Answer-** A hard cap refers to the upper limit of funds that a Cryptocurrency initiative seeks to secure during an Initial Coin Offering (ICO). Once this hard cap is achieved, the ICO concludes, and no further tokens are made available for sale. The establishment of a hard cap is intended to restrict the total investment amount and avert oversubscription, ensuring that the project does not accumulate more funds than it can effectively utilize.

## 34. Question- What is meant by a Soft Cap in an ICO?

**Answer-** A soft cap in an Initial Coin Offering (ICO) refers to the minimum funding target that a Cryptocurrency project must achieve to continue its development initiatives. Should the soft cap not be met, the project may be terminated, and typically, the funds will be refunded to the investors. This threshold is crucial as it ensures that the project has sufficient financial resources to be considered viable.

## 35. Question- What is meant by Stablecoin?
**Answer-** A stablecoin is a category of Cryptocurrency that is engineered to maintain a consistent value by being linked to a reserve asset, such as a fiat currency like the US dollar or a commodity such as gold. The primary objective of stablecoins is to offer stability and mitigate the volatility often associated with other cryptocurrencies. They are frequently utilized as a means of exchange and a reliable store of value within the Cryptocurrency ecosystem. Notable examples include Tether (USDT) and USD Coin (USDC).

## 36. Question- What is meant by Cryptocurrency Wallet Address?
**Answer-** A Cryptocurrency wallet address is a distinct alphanumeric sequence that designates the location for sending or receiving Cryptocurrency. This address is generated from the public key and acts as the endpoint for transactions. Each type of Cryptocurrency has its own specific address format, and it is essential for users to utilize the correct format corresponding to the Cryptocurrency in question.

## 37. Question- What is meant by Blockchain Explorer?
**Answer-** A blockchain explorer is an online platform that enables users to examine and search the blockchain for particular transactions, addresses, and blocks. It offers real-time insights into the blockchain's status and activities, including transaction histories, block information, and network metrics. Blockchain explorers are instrumental in tracking transactions, confirming balances, and assessing the overall health of the network.

## 38. Question- What is meant by Public Ledger?

**Answer-** A public ledger is a clear and unalterable record of all transactions conducted on a blockchain. It is open to public access, allowing all participants to verify the authenticity and history of transactions. The public ledger is upheld by nodes within the blockchain network, which collaboratively validate and document transactions in a decentralized fashion.

## 39. Question- What is meant by Token Burn?

**Answer-** Token burn is the procedure of irrevocably eliminating a specified quantity of Cryptocurrency tokens from circulation by transferring them to an unspendable address or destroying them. This practice is frequently employed to decrease the overall supply of tokens, which may enhance their value by fostering scarcity. Additionally, token burns can be utilized to modify the tokenomics of a project or to provide rewards to token holders.

## 40. Question- What is meant by Block Reward?

**Answer-** A block reward refers to the remuneration that miners earn for successfully incorporating a new block into the blockchain. This reward comprises two components: the newly minted Cryptocurrency, known as the block subsidy, and the transaction fees associated with the transactions contained within the block. The block reward serves as an incentive for miners to maintain network security and validate transactions. It is important to note that the value of the block reward may diminish over time, as evidenced by the halving events that occur in Bitcoin.

## 41. Question- What is meant by Smart Contract Audit?

**Answer-** A smart contract audit entails a thorough examination of the code within a smart contract to detect any vulnerabilities, bugs, or potential security risks. Auditors meticulously review the code to confirm that it operates as intended and is free from flaws that could be exploited. Such audits are essential for projects that manage substantial amounts of Cryptocurrency or engage in sensitive operations, as they help avert costly errors and ensure the dependability of the contract.

## 42. Question- What is meant by Initial Coin Offering (ICO)?

**Answer-** An Initial Coin Offering (ICO) is a method of fundraising in which a nascent Cryptocurrency project offers its tokens to early investors in exchange for established cryptocurrencies like Bitcoin or Ethereum. ICOs are utilized to generate capital for the development of the project and typically involve selling tokens at a reduced price prior to their availability on exchanges. However, ICOs carry inherent risks due to their lower regulatory oversight, and it is imperative for investors to perform comprehensive research before engaging in such offerings.

## 43. Question- What is meant by Initial Exchange Offering (IEO)?

**Answer-** An Initial Exchange Offering (IEO) is a fundraising approach akin to an Initial Coin Offering (ICO), but it is executed through a Cryptocurrency exchange. In this model, the exchange serves as an intermediary, performing due diligence on the project and facilitating the sale of its tokens to users on its platform. IEOs are perceived as more secure than ICOs due to the additional layer of vetting and trust provided by the exchange. Participants can purchase tokens directly via the exchange, which frequently offers supplementary features such as integrated trading options.

## 44. Question- What is meant by Security Token Offering (STO)?

**Answer-** A Security Token Offering (STO) is a fundraising strategy in which tokens that signify ownership or other rights in a company or asset are offered to investors. In contrast to ICOs, which typically involve utility tokens, STOs focus on security tokens that are subject to regulatory scrutiny. This method provides enhanced regulatory compliance and investor protection, as security tokens are structured to adhere to securities laws and regulations.

## 45. Question- What is meant by Utility Token?
**Answer-** A utility token is a category of Cryptocurrency that grants access to a product or service within a designated blockchain-based platform. Unlike security tokens, utility tokens do not confer ownership or investment stakes in a company. Instead, they are utilized to pay for services, gain access to features, or engage in the platform's ecosystem. Examples include tokens used for transaction fee payments, accessing decentralized applications (dApps), or participating in governance activities.

## 46. Question- What is meant by Security Token?
**Answer-** A security token is a form of Cryptocurrency that signifies ownership or entitlements in a company or asset, akin to conventional securities such as stocks or bonds. These tokens are regulated and must adhere to securities legislation. They afford investors legal rights and protections, including dividend distributions and voting privileges, and are commonly utilized in Security Token Offerings (STOs).

## 47. Question- What is meant by dApp (Decentralized Application)?
**Answer-** A dApp, or Decentralized Application, is an application that operates on a decentralized network, such as a blockchain, instead of relying on a centralized server. dApps utilize smart contracts to perform their functions and engage with the blockchain. They provide advantages such as enhanced security, transparency, and resistance to censorship when compared to traditional applications. Notable examples of dApps include decentralized finance (DeFi) platforms and decentralized exchanges (DEXs).

**48. Question- What is meant by Cryptocurrency Fork?**
**Answer-** A Cryptocurrency fork is defined as a modification in a blockchain's protocol that may lead to the establishment of a new blockchain. Forks can be categorized into hard forks and soft forks. A hard fork results in a new blockchain that is incompatible with the original, while a soft fork represents a change that remains backward-compatible. Forks can arise for various reasons, including community disagreements or the introduction of new features.

**49. Question- What is meant by Blockchain Protocol?**
**Answer-** A blockchain protocol refers to a comprehensive framework of rules and standards that dictate the functioning of a blockchain network. This encompasses the consensus mechanism, the format of transactions, and the communication protocols that nodes utilize to interact and uphold the integrity of the blockchain. The protocol guarantees that all participants adhere to uniform regulations, thereby ensuring the security, consistency, and operational efficacy of the blockchain.

**50. Question- What is meant by a Timestamp in Blockchain?**
**Answer-** A timestamp in the context of blockchain serves as a precise record indicating the moment a transaction or block is incorporated into the blockchain. It plays a crucial role in preserving the chronological sequence of transactions and blocks, thereby ensuring the accuracy and immutability of the blockchain's historical data. Timestamps are vital for confirming the order of transactions and mitigating potential issues such as double-spending.

**51. Question- What is meant by Custodial Wallet?**
**Answer-** A custodial wallet is a specific category of Cryptocurrency wallet in which a third party, such as an exchange or service provider, is responsible for holding and managing your private keys. This arrangement necessitates a level of trust in the custodian to safeguard your funds and facilitate transactions.

While custodial wallets provide convenience and often come with additional features, they require users to place their trust in the custodian regarding the security of their assets.

## 52. Question- What is meant by a Blockchain-based Voting System?

**Answer-** A blockchain-based voting system is an electoral framework that employs blockchain technology to securely document, authenticate, and count votes. By utilizing the immutability and transparency features of blockchain, these systems strive to improve the security, transparency, and integrity of the electoral process. Voters utilize digital identities to cast their votes, which are then recorded on a blockchain ledger, thereby preventing tampering and ensuring accurate outcomes.

## 53. Question- What is meant by Non-custodial Wallet?

**Answer-** A non-custodial wallet refers to a Cryptocurrency wallet that allows users to maintain complete control over their private keys. This implies that the user is accountable for the security and backup of these keys. Non-custodial wallets provide enhanced privacy and autonomy; however, they necessitate that users exercise caution in safeguarding their private keys to avert potential loss or theft.

## 54. Question- What is meant by Staking in Cryptocurrency?

**Answer-** Staking in the realm of Cryptocurrency is the process of engaging with a Proof of Stake (PoS) blockchain network by committing a specific quantity of Cryptocurrency to assist in network functions, such as transaction validation and network security. In exchange for their participation, stakeholders may receive rewards, typically in the form of additional Cryptocurrency. This practice is essential for upholding the network's integrity and can also serve as a source of passive income for those involved.

## 55. Question- What is meant by Mining Pool?

**Answer-** A mining pool is an assembly of Cryptocurrency miners who collaborate by merging their computational resources to enhance the chances of successfully mining a block. By joining forces, miners can tackle blocks more effectively and achieve a steadier flow of rewards. These rewards are allocated among the members based on their individual contributions to the collective mining power of the pool.

## 56. Question- What is meant by Rekt in Cryptocurrency Slang?

**Answer-** The term "rekt," which is a shorthand for "wrecked," refers to an individual who has suffered considerable financial losses within the Cryptocurrency market, often as a result of misguided investments or trading strategies. This term is frequently utilized in online Cryptocurrency forums to describe scenarios where investors incur significant monetary losses.

## 57. Question- What is meant by Whale in Cryptocurrency?

**Answer-** A whale refers to a person or organization that possesses a substantial quantity of Cryptocurrency, sufficient enough to sway market dynamics. The actions of whales, particularly large trades, can lead to notable price changes, and their movements are closely monitored by other market participants, as they may indicate potential shifts in market trends.

## 58. Question- What is meant by Private Key?

**Answer-** A private key is a cryptographic code that grants access to Cryptocurrency held within a wallet. It plays a crucial role in authorizing transactions and verifying ownership of the funds linked to that key. It is imperative to maintain the security and confidentiality of private keys, as possession of the key allows control over the corresponding Cryptocurrency.

## 59. Question- What is meant by Public Key?
**Answer-** A public key is a cryptographic code utilized for receiving Cryptocurrency. It is generated from the private key and can be shared with others to facilitate the receipt of funds. The public key works in tandem with the private key to establish a unique address on the blockchain, enabling users to securely receive transactions.

## 60. Question- What is meant by Seed Phrase?
**Answer-** A seed phrase is a collection of words produced by a Cryptocurrency wallet that acts as a safeguard for recovering the wallet and its associated funds. This phrase serves as a human-readable form of the wallet's private keys and is essential for regaining access in the event that the wallet is lost or compromised. It is imperative to keep the seed phrase secure and confidential to avert unauthorized access.

## 61. Question- What is meant by Dust Transaction?
**Answer-** A dust transaction is defined as a transaction that involves an exceedingly small quantity of Cryptocurrency, often to the extent that the transaction fee surpasses the value of the amount being transferred. Such transactions may serve various functions, including dusting attacks, where minimal amounts are dispatched to numerous addresses to monitor and scrutinize wallet activities.

## 62. Question- What is meant by a Fork in Blockchain?
**Answer-** A fork in blockchain terminology signifies a modification or divergence in the protocol of the blockchain, leading to a division or update within the blockchain network. There are primarily two categories of forks: hard forks, which result in a new, incompatible version of the blockchain, and soft forks, which entail changes that remain compatible with previous versions. Forks may arise to facilitate upgrades, address disputes, or introduce new functionalities.

### 63. Question- What is meant by Pump and Dump Scheme?

**Answer-** A pump and dump scheme is a deceptive tactic in which the value of a Cryptocurrency is artificially boosted (pumped) through the dissemination of false or misleading information to lure in investors. Once the price reaches a certain level, the individuals behind the scheme sell off their assets (dump), resulting in a price collapse and significant losses for other investors. While such schemes are illegal in traditional financial markets, they are more challenging to regulate within the Cryptocurrency sector.

### 64. Question- What is meant by Multisig Wallet?

**Answer-** A multisig wallet, or multi-signature wallet, is a specific type of Cryptocurrency wallet that necessitates multiple private keys for transaction authorization. This feature provides an additional layer of security, ensuring that no individual can transfer funds without the consent of others. Multisig wallets are frequently employed by organizations or groups to bolster security measures and mitigate the risk of unauthorized access.

### 65. Question- What is meant by Testnet?

**Answer-** A testnet is an independent blockchain network designed specifically for testing and development activities. It replicates the main blockchain (mainnet) but utilizes test cryptocurrencies, enabling developers to trial new functionalities, conduct experiments, and detect potential issues without impacting the operational network. Testnets play a crucial role in ensuring that modifications and updates are reliable prior to their deployment on the mainnet.

### 66. Question- What is meant by Centralized Exchange (CEX)?

**Answer-** A centralized exchange (CEX) is a Cryptocurrency trading platform that operates under the oversight of a central authority or intermediary. CEXs facilitate the trading process by coordinating buy and sell orders and managing users' funds in their custody. They typically provide high liquidity, intuitive user interfaces, and a range of additional features; however, they may pose greater security risks and necessitate that users place their trust in the exchange to safeguard their funds.

## 67. Question- What is meant by Gas Fee?

**Answer-** A gas fee refers to the transaction cost incurred by users to compensate network participants, such as miners or validators, for their role in processing and confirming transactions on a blockchain. In the case of Ethereum, these fees are denominated in Ether (ETH) and serve to reward miners for their computational efforts. The amount of gas fee can fluctuate depending on the level of network congestion and the intricacy of the transaction.

## 68. Question- What is meant by Consensus Algorithm?

**Answer-** A consensus algorithm is a set of rules employed by blockchain networks to ensure agreement on the legitimacy of transactions and the current state of the ledger. This mechanism guarantees that all nodes within the network maintain a consistent version of the blockchain. Notable examples of consensus algorithms include Proof of Work (PoW), Proof of Stake (PoS), and Byzantine Fault Tolerance (BFT).

## 69. Question- What is meant by a Hard Fork in Blockchain?

**Answer-** A hard fork represents a major and incompatible alteration to a blockchain's protocol, resulting in the establishment of a new blockchain. In contrast to soft forks, which maintain backward compatibility, hard forks lead to a division within the blockchain network, creating two distinct chains with their own rules and cryptocurrencies. Such forks typically arise from disputes within the community or the implementation of significant upgrades.

**70. Question- What is meant by a Soft Fork in Blockchain?**
**Answer-** A soft fork in blockchain refers to an update to the protocol that is compatible with previous versions, allowing for the introduction of new rules or modifications without the necessity of creating a separate blockchain. Nodes that have not adopted the updated protocol can still validate transactions, although they may not be able to utilize the new features fully. This approach facilitates gradual enhancements and modifications while ensuring ongoing compatibility with the existing network.

**71. Question- What is meant by Tokenomics?**
**Answer-** Tokenomics is the study of the economic framework and design of a Cryptocurrency or token, which includes its supply, distribution, and incentive structures. It covers various elements such as the total number of tokens available, their allocation, utility, and the mechanisms that create scarcity or reward token holders. A comprehensive understanding of tokenomics is essential for assessing the potential value and long-term viability of a Cryptocurrency.

**72. Question- What is meant by Blockchain Smart Contract?**
**Answer-** A blockchain smart contract is defined as a self-executing agreement where the terms are encoded directly into the software. These contracts automatically enforce and execute their provisions when specific conditions are satisfied. Operating on blockchain platforms such as Ethereum, smart contracts offer a decentralized and trustless method for executing transactions and managing contractual agreements.

**73. Question- What is meant by Oracle in Blockchain?**
**Answer-** An oracle in the context of blockchain refers to a service that supplies external data to smart contracts. It serves as a conduit between the blockchain and real-world information, enabling smart contracts to access data from various external sources, such as market prices, weather data, or the results of

events. Oracles are essential for the functionality of sophisticated and data-reliant smart contract applications.

## 74. Question- What is meant by Liquidity Pool?
**Answer-** A liquidity pool is defined as a collection of assets contributed by users to a decentralized finance (DeFi) protocol, which aids in trading on decentralized exchanges (DEXs) and other DeFi platforms. These pools ensure that there is sufficient liquidity for users to trade assets without depending on a centralized order book. In exchange for their contributions, liquidity providers receive fees or rewards generated from the trading activities within the pool.

## 75. Question- What is meant by an Airdrop in Cryptocurrency?
**Answer-** An airdrop in the realm of Cryptocurrency is a promotional tactic that involves distributing free tokens or cryptocurrencies to a wide audience, typically aimed at raising awareness for a new project. Airdrops may be allocated to current holders of a specific Cryptocurrency, members of a community, or individuals who fulfill certain criteria. This strategy is effective in fostering interest and encouraging the adoption of new initiatives.

## 76. Question- What is meant by a Decentralized Finance (DeFi) Platform?
**Answer-** A decentralized finance (DeFi) platform refers to a financial system built on blockchain technology that functions independently of conventional intermediaries such as banks or brokers. These platforms utilize smart contracts and blockchain infrastructure to provide a variety of financial services, including lending, borrowing, trading, and interest generation. The primary objective of DeFi is to establish an open, permissionless, and transparent financial environment that is accessible to anyone with internet connectivity.

## 77. Question- What is meant by Cryptocurrency Halving Event?

**Answer-** A Cryptocurrency halving event signifies a predetermined decrease in the rewards allocated to miners for validating transactions. This event takes place at designated intervals or specific block heights and serves to regulate the issuance of new coins while mitigating inflation. For instance, Bitcoin experiences a halving approximately every four years, which reduces the block reward by fifty percent, thereby influencing the overall supply and market value of the Cryptocurrency.

## 78. Question- What is meant by Tokenized Asset?

**Answer-** A tokenized asset is defined as a tangible asset from the physical world, such as real estate, artwork, or commodities, that is represented by a digital token on a blockchain. The process of tokenization facilitates fractional ownership, enhances transferability, and increases the liquidity of traditional assets. Tokenized assets are managed and traded through blockchain technology, which ensures transparency and efficiency in the transactions involving these assets.

## 79. Question- What is meant by Blockchain Validator?

**Answer-** A blockchain validator is an entity within a blockchain network tasked with the verification and validation of transactions and blocks. These validators are essential for upholding the integrity and security of the blockchain. In consensus mechanisms such as Proof of Stake (PoS), validators are chosen based on their stake or other established criteria and receive rewards for their contributions.

## 80. Question- What is meant by a Sidechain in Blockchain?

**Answer-** A sidechain is an independent blockchain that operates alongside the primary blockchain (mainnet) and is engineered to interact with it via a two-way peg. Sidechains facilitate experimentation, enhance scalability, and allow for the introduction of new features without disrupting the main blockchain. They contribute to the overall performance of the network and provide additional capabilities.

## 81. Question- What is meant by Blockchain Scalability Issue?

**Answer-** A blockchain scalability issue pertains to the difficulty of enhancing the transaction throughput and capacity of a blockchain network while preserving decentralization and security. These issues emerge when the network is unable to accommodate an increasing volume of transactions, resulting in delayed processing times and elevated fees. Potential solutions to scalability challenges include network enhancements, layer-2 solutions, and alternative consensus protocols.

## 82. Question- What is meant by a Privacy Coin?

**Answer-** A privacy coin refers to a category of Cryptocurrency specifically designed to protect user privacy and anonymity by concealing transaction information and user identities. These coins employ various methods, including encryption, stealth addresses, and ring signatures, to maintain the confidentiality and untraceability of transaction data. Notable examples of privacy coins are Monero (XMR) and Zcash (ZEC).

## 83. Question- What is meant by Blockchain DAO (Decentralized Autonomous Organization)?

**Answer-** A blockchain DAO, or Decentralized Autonomous Organization, is an entity that operates under the governance of smart contracts and blockchain technology, with decision-making facilitated through decentralized voting by token holders. DAOs function without conventional management frameworks and strive to offer a transparent, democratic, and automated approach to managing projects, funds, or communities.

### 84. Question- What is meant by Blockchain Hash Function?

**Answer-** A blockchain hash function is a cryptographic algorithm that produces a fixed-size output (hash) from an input of any size. These hash functions are integral to blockchain networks, as they secure data, generate unique identifiers for blocks, and uphold data integrity. They are essential for the immutability and security of the blockchain, since even a minor alteration in the input leads to a significantly different hash.

### 85. Question- What is meant by Cross-chain Transaction?

**Answer-** A cross-chain transaction is defined as the movement of assets or information between distinct blockchain networks. This type of transaction promotes interoperability and facilitates communication among various blockchains, enabling the transfer of assets or data across different platforms. Mechanisms such as atomic swaps, bridge protocols, and interoperability solutions are essential for executing cross-chain transactions.

### 86. Question- What is meant by Blockchain Consensus Mechanism?

**Answer-** A blockchain consensus mechanism is a set of rules designed to ensure that all nodes within a network reach a consensus regarding the legitimacy of transactions and the current state of the blockchain. This mechanism guarantees that every participant maintains a consistent version of the ledger, thereby mitigating problems like double-spending. Notable consensus mechanisms include Proof of Work (PoW), Proof of Stake (PoS), and Byzantine Fault Tolerance (BFT).

### 87. Question- What is meant by Blockchain Protocol Upgrade?

**Answer-** A blockchain protocol upgrade involves modifications or enhancements to the established rules and standards that govern a blockchain network. These upgrades can be executed through hard forks or soft forks and are intended to improve the network's performance, security, or scalability. Typically, protocol upgrades are suggested and evaluated by the community prior to their implementation.

## 88. Question- What is meant by Token Burn?
**Answer-** A token burn refers to the irreversible process of eliminating a specific quantity of Cryptocurrency tokens from circulation. This action is typically undertaken to decrease the overall supply of a token, thereby enhancing its scarcity and potentially increasing its market value. The tokens that are burned are transferred to a wallet that lacks a private key, making them permanently inaccessible.

## 89. Question- What is meant by Blockchain Checkpoint?
**Answer-** A blockchain checkpoint is a specific block or reference point within the blockchain that is recognized as valid and serves as a benchmark for subsequent blocks. These checkpoints enhance the efficiency and security of blockchain networks by facilitating the rapid verification of the blockchain's integrity, thereby mitigating the risks of forks or invalid transactions.

## 90. Question- What is meant by Decentralized Identity (DID)?
**Answer-** A decentralized identity (DID) represents a digital identity that is governed and controlled by the individual rather than a centralized entity. Utilizing blockchain technology, DIDs enable the secure and decentralized management of identities, empowering users to oversee their personal information and share it selectively. The primary objectives of DIDs are to improve privacy, security, and user autonomy.

## 91. Question- What is meant by Blockchain-based Marketplace?
**Answer-** A blockchain-based marketplace refers to an online platform that leverages blockchain technology to enable the buying, selling, and trading of various goods and services. These marketplaces provide advantages such as enhanced transparency,

improved security, and a diminished need for intermediaries. They encompass a range of marketplace types, including decentralized exchanges, NFT marketplaces, and peer-to-peer trading platforms.

## 92. Question- What is meant by Token Swap?
**Answer-** A token swap is defined as the act of exchanging one Cryptocurrency or token for another, typically prompted by modifications in a project's technology or protocol. Such swaps may take place during specific events like token migrations, upgrades, or conversions. They can be executed either manually by users or automatically through the use of smart contracts or exchanges.

## 93. Question- What is meant by Blockchain Node?
**Answer-** A blockchain node is characterized as a computer or device that engages in the blockchain network by preserving a copy of the blockchain ledger, validating transactions, and disseminating information to other nodes. Nodes are essential to the network's security and consensus, as they ensure the legitimacy of transactions and maintain synchronization across the blockchain network.

## 94. Question- What is meant by Blockchain Ledger?
**Answer-** A blockchain ledger refers to a digital repository that records all transactions and data within a blockchain network. It is composed of a series of blocks, each containing a collection of transactions, and is upheld by the nodes of the network. This ledger is characterized by its decentralized and immutable nature, which guarantees the accuracy, security, and resistance to tampering or fraudulent activities of the transaction history.

## 95. Question- What is meant by Blockchain Transaction Fee?
**Answer-** A blockchain transaction fee is a charge incurred by users to compensate network participants, such as miners or

validators, for their role in processing and confirming transactions on the blockchain. These fees fluctuate based on various factors, including network congestion, the size of the transaction, and the specific blockchain protocol in use. Transaction fees serve as an incentive for network participants to prioritize and validate transactions, thereby facilitating the efficient functioning of the blockchain.

**96. Question- What is meant by Blockchain Fork?**
**Answer-** A blockchain fork represents a modification or divergence in the protocol of a blockchain, leading to the establishment of a new blockchain or alterations to the existing one. Forks can be categorized into hard forks and soft forks, based on whether they result in the creation of a new blockchain or maintain backward compatibility. Such forks may arise for numerous reasons, including the implementation of upgrades, the resolution of disputes, or the introduction of new functionalities.

**97. Question- What is meant by Blockchain Smart Contract Audit?**
**Answer-** A blockchain smart contract audit refers to a comprehensive examination of the code and operational aspects of a smart contract, aimed at uncovering vulnerabilities, errors, and potential concerns. Such audits are performed by security professionals or specialized firms to confirm that the smart contract functions as intended, is safeguarded against attacks, and complies with established best practices. These audits are essential for preserving the integrity and dependability of smart contracts within blockchain applications.

**98. Question- What is meant by Decentralized Exchange (DEX) Aggregator?**
**Answer-** A decentralized exchange (DEX) aggregator is a platform or tool that aggregates and compares pricing from various decentralized exchanges to identify the most advantageous trading rates for users. DEX aggregators facilitate traders in

accessing improved liquidity and minimizing slippage by directing their orders to the most favorable exchange or liquidity pool. They enhance the trading experience and increase efficiency by providing a unified overview of available trading options.

## 99. Question- What is meant by Cryptocurrency trading?

**Answer-** Cryptocurrency trading encompasses the activities of purchasing, selling, or exchanging digital currencies such as Bitcoin, Ethereum, and others on various online platforms known as exchanges. Traders seek to generate profits by forecasting the future movements of Cryptocurrency values.

**Several methods of Cryptocurrency trading:**
**Spot Trading-** Involves the direct purchase of a Cryptocurrency, which is then held until its value appreciates, allowing for a profitable sale.
**Day Trading-** Characterized by the frequent buying and selling of cryptocurrencies within a single day to take advantage of short-term price fluctuations.
**Margin Trading-** Enables traders to borrow capital to increase their potential profits (or losses).
**Futures Trading-** Entails entering into contracts to buy or sell a Cryptocurrency at a specified future date for a predetermined price.
**Arbitrage-** Involves acquiring Cryptocurrency on one exchange at a lower price and subsequently selling it on another exchange where the price is higher.

## 100. Question- What is the Primary Objective of Cryptocurrency Trading?

**Answer-** The primary objective of Cryptocurrency trading is to capitalize on price variations by employing strategies such as technical analysis, monitoring market trends, and staying informed about economic developments. Given the high volatility of cryptocurrencies, trading can present both significant rewards and considerable risks.

# 25 Legal and Illegal Aspects

Chapter- 2: 25 main legal and 25 main illegal aspects of Cryptocurrency as of 2024, explained in a simple language:

## Legal Aspects

**1. Regulatory Compliance:** Numerous nations mandate that Cryptocurrency enterprises adhere to financial regulations, including anti-money laundering (AML) and know-your-customer (KYC) protocols. This framework is designed to deter illicit activities and safeguard consumers.

**2. Tax Reporting:** In various jurisdictions, transactions involving cryptocurrencies are liable for taxation. Users are obligated to declare their profits and losses to tax authorities, and many exchanges offer tools to facilitate tax reporting.

**3. Securities Regulation:** Certain cryptocurrencies and tokens are categorized as securities, necessitating compliance with securities legislation. This classification requires them to fulfill specific regulatory obligations prior to public offering.

**4. Consumer Protection:** Regulations may compel Cryptocurrency firms to adopt measures aimed at consumer protection, such as secure fund storage and transparent operational practices.

**5. Licensing:** In numerous areas, Cryptocurrency exchanges and related businesses are required to secure licenses for lawful operation. This process ensures compliance with local laws and regulations.

**6. Data Privacy:** Cryptocurrencies frequently need to adhere to data protection laws, such as the General Data Protection Regulation (GDPR) in Europe, which regulates the collection and utilization of personal data.

**7. Intellectual Property Rights:** Cryptocurrencies and blockchain innovations can be safeguarded under intellectual property legislation, encompassing patents, copyrights, and trademarks.

**8. Consumer Education:** Legal frameworks often highlight the importance of educating consumers regarding the risks linked to cryptocurrencies, including market fluctuations and security vulnerabilities.

**9. Anti-Fraud Measures:** Regulations necessitate that Cryptocurrency businesses establish anti-fraud protocols to defend against scams and fraudulent activities.

**10. Financial Stability:** Certain nations keep a close watch on cryptocurrencies to ensure they do not threaten the overall financial system and take steps to alleviate any potential risks.

**11. AML Compliance:** Numerous jurisdictions mandate that Cryptocurrency enterprises adopt anti-money laundering (AML) protocols, which include monitoring transactions and reporting any suspicious activities.

**12. KYC Requirements:** Regulations pertaining to know-your-customer (KYC) necessitate that Cryptocurrency exchanges authenticate the identities of their users to avert fraud and unlawful activities.

**13. Legal Tender Status:** In various countries, cryptocurrencies may be acknowledged as legal tender, allowing them to be utilized for transactions and payments similarly to conventional currencies.

**14. Cross-Border Transactions:** Legal frameworks frequently address the regulation and taxation of cross-border transactions involving cryptocurrencies.

**15. Bank Integration:** Certain nations have established regulations permitting banks to provide Cryptocurrency services, such as custody and trading, under defined conditions.

**16. Smart Contract Legality:** Smart contracts, which are agreements executed automatically through code, are increasingly being recognized as legally enforceable in numerous jurisdictions.

**17. Regulated Custodians:** Regulations may stipulate that Cryptocurrency custodians comply with specific standards for the secure storage of digital assets.

**18. Investment Protection:** Legislation may require investment firms engaged with cryptocurrencies to follow rules aimed at safeguarding investors, including disclosure obligations and equitable trading practices.

**19. Anti-Terrorism Financing:** Regulations are designed to prevent the use of cryptocurrencies for financing terrorism and other illicit activities by monitoring transactions and reporting any suspicious activities.

**20. Blockchain Data Integrity:** Legal systems acknowledge the unchangeable and transparent nature of blockchain data, which can serve as evidence in judicial proceedings.

**21. Regulatory Sandboxes:** Certain jurisdictions implement regulatory sandboxes that enable Cryptocurrency enterprises to trial their products and services while under the oversight of regulatory authorities.

**22. Consumer Dispute Resolution:** Legal frameworks may establish processes for addressing conflicts between consumers and Cryptocurrency enterprises, which can include arbitration and mediation options.

**23. Regulatory Guidance:** Numerous countries offer regulatory guidance regarding the treatment of cryptocurrencies, assisting businesses and users in comprehending their legal responsibilities.

**24. Insurance Requirements:** Some regulations mandate that Cryptocurrency enterprises maintain insurance coverage to safeguard against losses resulting from cyberattacks or other incidents.

**25. Compliance Audits:** Cryptocurrency enterprises may be required to undergo periodic audits to verify their adherence to legal and regulatory standards.

Illegal Aspects

**1. Deceptive Practices:** Activities such as Ponzi schemes, fraudulent initial coin offerings (ICOs), and phishing scams involve dishonest methods aimed at misappropriating funds from investors.

**2. Concealment of Illicit Funds:** Utilizing cryptocurrencies to obscure the source of illegally acquired money and to present it as legitimate is prohibited in numerous jurisdictions.

**3. Financing of Terrorism:** The use of cryptocurrencies to support terrorist operations is forbidden and carries significant legal repercussions.

**4. Tax Noncompliance:** Neglecting to declare Cryptocurrency profits or losses for taxation purposes is unlawful and may lead to penalties and legal ramifications.

**5. Unauthorized Exchanges:** Running a Cryptocurrency exchange without the necessary licenses and regulatory approvals is illegal in various nations.

**6. Price Manipulation Schemes:** Influencing the value of a Cryptocurrency through deceptive or misleading information to benefit from artificially inflated prices is against the law.

**7. Insider Trading:** Engaging in Cryptocurrency transactions based on confidential information, such as undisclosed developments or news, is both illegal and unethical.

**8. Cyber Theft:** Gaining unauthorized access to Cryptocurrency wallets or exchanges to misappropriate funds constitutes a criminal act.

**9. Unregistered Financial Instruments:** Promoting cryptocurrencies or tokens that are deemed securities without appropriate registration or compliance is illegal.

**10. Illicit Gambling:** Utilizing cryptocurrencies to engage in or facilitate unlawful gambling activities can result in legal complications.

**11. Extortion via Ransomware:** Requiring payment in Cryptocurrency for the release of data or systems held hostage by ransomware is illegal and regarded as extortion.

**12. Fraudulent ICOs:** Initiating an initial coin offering (ICO) with misleading claims regarding the project or its potential to mislead investors is a criminal offense.

**13. Unregistered Investment Advising:** Offering investment guidance or managing Cryptocurrency assets without the necessary registration or licensing constitutes an illegal activity.

**14. Spoofing and Front Running:** Participating in market manipulation practices such as spoofing (submitting fictitious orders) or front running (executing trades based on confidential information) is prohibited by law.

**15. Dark Web Transactions:** Engaging in illegal transactions using cryptocurrencies on dark web platforms, including the purchase of drugs or illicit services, is unlawful.

**16. Regulatory Evasion:** Circumventing compliance with regulations, such as Anti-Money Laundering (AML) or Know Your Customer (KYC) requirements, by operating in jurisdictions with lenient laws is illegal.

**17. Unauthorized Access:** Illegally accessing Cryptocurrency accounts, private keys, or confidential information is a criminal offense.

**18. Selling Unregistered Tokens:** The sale of tokens that have not been duly registered or authorized by regulatory bodies is against the law.

**19. False Advertising:** Making misleading statements regarding a Cryptocurrency's characteristics, advantages, or investment potential to lure investors is classified as fraud.

**20. Coin Laundering:** Engaging in intricate transactions to conceal the source of stolen or unlawfully acquired Cryptocurrency is illegal.

**21. Phishing Scams:** Attempting to unlawfully acquire Cryptocurrency through phishing schemes, where individuals are deceived into disclosing private information, is illegal.

**22. Exploiting Vulnerabilities:** Taking advantage of software weaknesses to gain unauthorized access or manipulate Cryptocurrency systems is a criminal act.

**23. Impersonation Scams:** Falsely representing oneself as a credible individual or organization to trick people into surrendering their Cryptocurrency is illegal.

**24. Unauthorized Token Sales:** Carrying out token sales without the necessary authorization or adherence to regulatory standards is against the law.

**25. Unlawful Use of Blockchain Technology:** Employing blockchain technology for illicit purposes, such as the creation and distribution of malware, constitutes criminal behavior.

These elements illustrate the dynamic landscape of Cryptocurrency regulation and enforcement as of 2024. Legal structures are being established to tackle emerging challenges and to guarantee that Cryptocurrency is utilized in a responsible manner and in compliance with legal standards.

Chapter- 3: 50 points on "Why it is safe to invest in Cryptocurrency" and 50 points on "Why it is unsafe to invest in Cryptocurrency" in easy and simple way.

The following 50 points outline the reasons why investing in Cryptocurrency can be considered safe:

**1. Diversification:** Incorporating cryptocurrencies into your investment portfolio can help mitigate risk by spreading it across various asset classes. If one investment declines in value, others may compensate, thereby stabilizing your overall risk profile. For example, while traditional stocks may experience downturns, your Cryptocurrency holdings could potentially thrive.

**2. High Potential Returns:** Certain cryptocurrencies, such as Bitcoin and Ethereum, have experienced significant appreciation in value over time. This potential for substantial returns can be more attractive compared to conventional investments that typically yield lower growth.

**3. Global Accessibility:** Cryptocurrencies can be accessed by anyone with an internet connection, enabling individuals from various countries to invest, trade, and engage in the global market. This accessibility creates investment opportunities for those who may lack access to traditional financial systems.

**4. Blockchain Technology:** The underlying technology of cryptocurrencies, known as blockchain, provides a secure and transparent record of all transactions. Once a transaction is entered into the blockchain, it cannot be modified or tampered with, ensuring the reliability of the information.

**5. Decentralization:** Many cryptocurrencies function on decentralized networks, meaning they are not governed by a single entity or government. This characteristic diminishes the likelihood of manipulation or interference from central authorities, enhancing the system's robustness.

**6. Innovation:** Investing in cryptocurrencies allows you to engage with pioneering technologies and emerging projects that have the potential to transform various sectors, including finance and supply chain management. This innovation can foster significant growth and create new investment opportunities.

**7. Liquidity:** Prominent cryptocurrencies such as Bitcoin and Ethereum are available on numerous exchanges, facilitating the buying and selling process without causing significant price fluctuations. The presence of high liquidity allows for the swift conversion of investments into cash when necessary.

**8. 24/7 Market:** In contrast to conventional stock markets that function solely during business hours, Cryptocurrency markets operate continuously, 24 hours a day, seven days a week. This round-the-clock availability enables you to trade and manage your investments at your convenience, enhancing your flexibility and control.

**9. Transparency:** Transactions conducted on a blockchain are publicly documented and accessible, ensuring a high level of transparency. This feature allows for the verification of transactions and the tracing of fund movements, thereby increasing accountability within the system.

**10. Ownership Control:** By possessing Cryptocurrency, you have direct control over your assets through private keys, which are cryptographic tools that grant you access to and management of your funds. This autonomy diminishes your dependence on banks or other third-party entities.

**11. Low Barriers to Entry:** Entering the Cryptocurrency market can be relatively affordable compared to other investment avenues. Many cryptocurrencies can be purchased in fractional amounts, making them accessible even to those with limited financial resources.

**12. Security Measures:** Cryptocurrency exchanges and wallets frequently implement sophisticated security protocols, including encryption and multi-factor authentication, to safeguard your assets against unauthorized access and cyber threats.

**13. Regulatory Progress:** Numerous governments are actively developing clearer regulations surrounding cryptocurrencies, which can enhance investor protection and promote a fairer and more transparent market environment.

**14. Institutional Adoption:** A growing number of major corporations and institutional investors are allocating funds to cryptocurrencies, which contributes to the market's credibility and stability. Their involvement may foster greater mainstream acceptance and legitimacy.

**15. Cross-Border Transactions:** Cryptocurrencies facilitate the swift and efficient transfer of funds across international borders, eliminating the necessity for conventional intermediaries such as banks. This capability can lead to a reduction in transaction costs and shorter processing durations.

**16. Smart Contracts:** These are automated agreements with their stipulations encoded directly into software. They autonomously enforce and execute the terms of the contract without requiring intermediaries, which can result in decreased expenses and enhanced operational efficiency.

**17. Diversified Use Cases:** Cryptocurrencies serve a multitude of functions beyond mere investment. They are utilized in various sectors, including payments, decentralized finance (DeFi), and digital collectibles (NFTs), thereby offering numerous pathways for expansion.

**18. Anonymity and Privacy:** Certain cryptocurrencies provide features that bolster user privacy, enabling transactions to be carried out with a higher degree of anonymity compared to conventional financial systems.

**19. Market Maturity:** The Cryptocurrency market has developed and matured, characterized by improved infrastructure, sophisticated trading tools, and enhanced operational practices. This evolution contributes to a more stable and dependable market landscape.

**20. Community Support:** Numerous Cryptocurrency initiatives benefit from robust and engaged communities that play a crucial role in their development and success. This communal backing can foster innovation and offer essential resources and insights.

**21. Educational Resources:** A wealth of resources is available for investors seeking to understand cryptocurrencies, including online courses, discussion forums, and research publications. Such educational tools can empower individuals to make well-informed investment choices.

**22. Diverse Investment Options:** The Cryptocurrency ecosystem encompasses a variety of asset types, including numerous coins, tokens, and blockchain initiatives. This variety enables investors to engage in sectors that resonate with their interests and risk profiles.

**23. Liquidity Providers:** Decentralized exchanges utilize liquidity pools to facilitate trading activities. These pools ensure the availability of liquidity, thereby enabling smooth transaction execution, even for assets that are less widely traded.

**24. Tokenization of Assets:** Cryptocurrencies facilitate the development of digital tokens that symbolize tangible assets, such as real estate or artwork. This innovation can enhance the accessibility and affordability of investing in these assets.

**25. Regulatory Sandboxes:** Certain nations have established regulatory sandboxes, which serve as controlled environments for testing new Cryptocurrency initiatives under regulatory oversight. This approach ensures that emerging innovations adhere to legal requirements.

**26. Integration with Traditional Finance:** Numerous conventional financial institutions are now providing Cryptocurrency-related services, including trading and custody solutions. This integration serves to connect traditional finance with the realm of digital assets.

**27. Access to DeFi:** Decentralized finance (DeFi) platforms present novel financial services, such as lending and borrowing, without the need for traditional intermediaries. These platforms can offer appealing returns and enhanced control over one's assets.

**28. Transparency in Code:** A significant number of Cryptocurrency projects are open-source, allowing their code to be publicly accessible for examination. This level of transparency enables developers and auditors to review and refine the code, thereby improving security and fostering trust.

**29. Secure Storage Options:** Sophisticated storage solutions, including hardware wallets, provide a secure method for storing cryptocurrencies offline, safeguarding them against online threats.

**30. Professional Services:** Financial advisors and asset managers are increasingly offering expertise on Cryptocurrency investments, delivering guidance and support to assist individuals in navigating the market.

**31. Technological Advancements:** Continuous progress in blockchain and cryptographic technologies enhances the security, efficiency, and scalability of cryptocurrencies, rendering them more robust and dependable.

**32. Diversified Market Segments:** The Cryptocurrency market encompasses various segments, including infrastructure projects, financial applications, and digital collectibles. This diversification offers a range of investment opportunities.

**33. Emerging Trends:** The advent of new trends and innovations, including decentralized autonomous organizations (DAOs) and decentralized applications (dApps), presents intriguing investment opportunities and the potential for significant growth.

**34. Strong Market Resilience:** Prominent cryptocurrencies have shown remarkable resilience during periods of market decline, managing to recover and sustain growth over time, which can instill confidence in long-term investors.

**35. Governance Participation:** Numerous Cryptocurrency initiatives incorporate community governance, enabling investors to engage in decision-making processes and influence the project's evolution.

**36. Increased Institutional Interest:** The participation of institutional investors, such as hedge funds and corporate treasuries, lends credibility to the Cryptocurrency market and may contribute to price stabilization.

**37. DeFi Yield Farming:** Engaging in yield farming and staking on decentralized finance (DeFi) platforms can provide avenues for earning rewards and interest on Cryptocurrency holdings, potentially enhancing returns.

**38. Enhanced Accessibility Tools:** Technological advancements, including intuitive wallets and trading platforms, facilitate easier management of Cryptocurrency assets for both novice and seasoned investors.

**39. Legal Frameworks:** Numerous nations are establishing legal frameworks for cryptocurrencies, offering clearer regulations and protections for investors, which aids in fostering a more stable market environment.

**40. Community Engagement:** Active and involved communities surrounding cryptocurrencies offer support, disseminate knowledge, and drive innovation, benefiting both investors and the wider ecosystem.

**41. Historical Growth:** Historical analysis indicates that certain cryptocurrencies, such as Bitcoin, have achieved significant long-term growth, underscoring their potential for future value enhancement.

**42. Innovative Financial Instruments:** Emerging financial instruments, including Cryptocurrency exchange-traded funds

(ETFs) and futures contracts, present new avenues for investing in digital assets with enhanced flexibility.

**43. Lower Transaction Expenses:** Cryptocurrencies can significantly reduce transaction expenses in comparison to conventional banking systems, particularly for international transfers, by removing intermediaries and associated fees.

**44. Growing Acceptance:** An increasing number of businesses and merchants are beginning to accept cryptocurrencies as a form of payment, which enhances their practical use and may further promote adoption and value.

**45. Functional Token Use:** Numerous cryptocurrencies serve specific purposes within their respective ecosystems, such as enabling access to services or facilitating governance participation, thereby providing functional value beyond mere investment.

**46. Streamlined Market Operations:** Contemporary trading platforms and technologies facilitate efficient and transparent market operations, simplifying the process of trading and managing Cryptocurrency investments.

**47. Network Dynamics:** The expanding user base and applications within the Cryptocurrency ecosystem generate network dynamics, potentially enhancing the value and utility of digital assets as the network grows.

**48. Opportunities for Early-Stage Investments:** Engaging in Cryptocurrency investments can open doors to early-stage projects and innovations that may not be accessible through traditional investment avenues.

**49. Decreased Reliance on Traditional Banking:** Cryptocurrencies present an alternative to conventional banking systems, empowering users to manage and transfer funds independently of centralized institutions.

**50. Promoting Financial Inclusion:** Cryptocurrencies can extend financial services to individuals who are underserved by traditional banking systems, creating new opportunities for economic engagement and development.

The following 50 points outline the reasons why investing in Cryptocurrency can be considered unsafe:

**1. Significant Price Fluctuations:** The prices of cryptocurrencies are known for their extreme volatility, often experiencing sharp changes within brief timeframes. Such fluctuations can result in considerable financial losses if the market trends unfavorably for your investments.

**2. Evolving Regulatory Environment:** The framework governing cryptocurrencies is still in a state of evolution, and unexpected alterations in laws or regulations can influence both the value and legality of your investments.

**3. Vulnerability to Security Breaches:** Despite advancements in security protocols, Cryptocurrency exchanges and wallets remain susceptible to hacking and cyber threats. Incidents of security breaches can lead to substantial financial losses.

**4. Insufficient Consumer Safeguards:** Cryptocurrencies typically do not offer the same level of consumer protection found in conventional financial systems. Recovering lost or stolen funds can prove to be challenging or even impossible.

**5. Presence of Fraudulent Activities:** The Cryptocurrency sector has been plagued by various scams and fraudulent schemes, including deceptive investment opportunities and Ponzi schemes, which can mislead investors and result in financial losses.

**6. Potential for Market Manipulation:** The Cryptocurrency market is vulnerable to manipulation by large investors or organized groups, which can distort pricing and undermine market integrity.

**7. Unregulated Trading Platforms:** Certain Cryptocurrency exchanges function without adequate regulation or oversight, heightening the risk of fraud, mismanagement, and financial loss.

**8. Technical Complexity:** The intricate nature of cryptocurrencies and blockchain technology can be challenging to comprehend, potentially leading to miscalculations and suboptimal investment decisions.

**9. Challenges with Liquidity:** While major cryptocurrencies tend to have high liquidity, smaller or newer cryptocurrencies may experience limited liquidity, complicating the buying or selling process without affecting their price.

**10. Legal Considerations:** Engaging in Cryptocurrency investments may entail legal risks, such as regulatory enforcement actions or disputes regarding the legality of specific activities, which can impact your investment.

**11. Insufficient Fundamental Value:** Numerous cryptocurrencies lack conventional revenue models or inherent value, complicating the evaluation of their long-term viability and stability.

**12. Fraudulent Investment Schemes:** The Cryptocurrency sector has been a target for deceptive investment schemes that guarantee substantial returns with minimal risk, often resulting in considerable financial losses.

**13. Technological Vulnerabilities:** Cryptocurrencies and their foundational technologies may contain flaws, weaknesses, or unexpected problems that could result in security breaches or operational disruptions.

**14. Governmental Restrictions:** Authorities may implement regulations or prohibitions on Cryptocurrency activities, adversely affecting the value of investments and the overall market.

**15. Market Volatility:** The Cryptocurrency market is characterized by extreme volatility, with sudden and unpredictable fluctuations that complicate the management and forecasting of investment outcomes.

**16. Limited Recovery Options:** In the event of fund loss due to hacking or exchange failures, recovery options may be scarce, leaving investors without recourse.

**17. Absence of Standardization:** The lack of uniform practices and protocols within the Cryptocurrency domain can result in inconsistencies and heightened risks for investors.

**18. Exaggerated Project Claims:** Numerous Cryptocurrency initiatives are promoted with inflated assertions and promises that may not materialize, potentially leading to losses for investors who were swayed by the hype.

**19. Uncertain Legal Status:** The legal classification of cryptocurrencies can be ambiguous or differ across jurisdictions, creating uncertainty and possible legal complications for investors.

**20. Risk of Obsolescence:** The swift evolution of technology in the Cryptocurrency arena means that current projects may rapidly become outdated as new innovations arise.

**21. Market Sentiment:** The prices of cryptocurrencies are frequently influenced by market sentiment and speculative trading activities, which can result in irrational price fluctuations and heightened investment risks.

**22. Lack of Transparency:** Certain Cryptocurrency initiatives may not offer adequate transparency concerning their operations, development processes, or financial health, complicating the assessment of their legitimacy.

**23. Operational Risks:** Cryptocurrency projects and platforms may encounter operational challenges, including technical malfunctions, poor management, or fraudulent activities, which can adversely affect their performance and valuation.

**24. Investment Bubble:** The Cryptocurrency market has witnessed speculative bubbles, during which prices become artificially inflated and detached from their intrinsic value, potentially resulting in market crashes and substantial financial losses.

**25. Legal Risks of Usage:** Engaging in Cryptocurrency transactions for illicit purposes or within unregulated environments can expose investors to legal repercussions and penalties, such as fines or legal proceedings.

**26. Scalability Issues:** Certain cryptocurrencies encounter difficulties related to scalability, which can hinder their performance and capacity to manage an increasing volume of transactions.

**27. Environmental Concerns:** Some cryptocurrencies, especially those utilizing energy-intensive proof-of-work (PoW) mechanisms, pose significant environmental challenges due to their substantial energy consumption.

**28. Lack of Insurance:** Unlike traditional bank accounts, Cryptocurrency assets are typically not insured, meaning that in cases of theft or loss, there may be no recourse for compensation.

**29. Counterparty Risk:** Investing in cryptocurrencies necessitates reliance on third-party platforms for transactions and asset custody, which introduces counterparty risk should these entities fail or become compromised.

**30. Market Speculation:** The Cryptocurrency market is characterized by high levels of speculation, with price movements often driven by hype and conjecture rather than fundamental economic factors, thereby increasing the likelihood of abrupt price shifts.

**31. Complex Taxation:** The taxation of Cryptocurrency transactions can be intricate and differ across jurisdictions, which may result in challenges related to tax compliance and reporting.

**32. Privacy Risks:** Although certain cryptocurrencies provide privacy features, others may reveal transaction details or user identities, raising potential privacy issues.

**33. Unstable Project Teams:** Cryptocurrency initiatives may be led by unstable or inexperienced teams, heightening the risk of project failure or mismanagement.

**34. Lack of Regulation:** The lack of comprehensive regulatory frameworks in certain regions can increase the likelihood of fraud, manipulation, and exploitation of investors.

**35. Potential for Hacks:** Cryptocurrency wallets and exchanges are often targeted by cybercriminals, and weaknesses in their security can lead to substantial financial losses.

**36. Uncertain Future:** The future prospects of many cryptocurrencies remain uncertain due to possible technological, regulatory, or market shifts that could affect their sustainability.

**37. Difficulty in Valuation:** Assessing the true value of a Cryptocurrency can be difficult due to the absence of conventional valuation metrics and differing perspectives on its worth.

**38. Volatile Market Sentiment:** Cryptocurrency prices are often highly reactive to news, rumors, and social media trends, resulting in extreme and unpredictable fluctuations.

**39. Potential for Fraudulent Activity:** The anonymity and decentralized characteristics of cryptocurrencies can be misused for fraudulent activities, including scams and illicit transactions.

**40. Limited Consumer Protections:** In contrast to traditional financial institutions, cryptocurrencies frequently lack consumer protection measures, complicating the resolution of disputes or recovery of losses.

**41. Operational Failures:** Cryptocurrency platforms and projects may encounter operational issues, including technical malfunctions or poor management, which can impact their performance and overall value.

**42. Changes in Regulation:** Abrupt modifications in regulatory frameworks or governmental policies can negatively influence Cryptocurrency investments and their legal standing.

**43. Projects with Low Market Capitalization:** Investing in cryptocurrencies that have a low market cap can be precarious, as they may exhibit insufficient liquidity, stability, or broad acceptance.

**44. Deceptive Information:** The Cryptocurrency sector is frequently inundated with misleading information and exaggerated claims, complicating the task for investors to differentiate between credible data and falsehoods.

**45. Fraudulent ICOs:** Initial Coin Offerings (ICOs) have been exploited to fund deceitful ventures, resulting in considerable financial losses for investors who relied on misleading information.

**46. Token Supply Challenges:** Cryptocurrencies with inadequately structured tokenomics or an excessive supply may encounter difficulties in maintaining value and ensuring market stability.

**47. Technical Complexity:** The intricate nature of Cryptocurrency technology and smart contracts can lead to confusion and mismanagement among investors.

**48. Changing Market Conditions:** The Cryptocurrency market is in a state of constant evolution, and staying abreast of technological advancements and regulatory changes can prove challenging for investors.

**49. Sensitivity to Market Sentiment:** Cryptocurrency valuations are often swayed by market sentiment and speculative trading, rendering them vulnerable to abrupt and unpredictable price changes.

**50. Absence of Historical Data:** As a relatively nascent asset class, cryptocurrencies do not possess a long-standing history of performance and stability, making them inherently more uncertain compared to traditional investment vehicles.

These comprehensive explanations are intended to enhance understanding of the risks and advantages associated with Cryptocurrency investments, thereby assisting investors in making more informed choices.

Chapter- 4: The following guidelines are designed to assist individuals in making responsible and informed decisions regarding Cryptocurrency investments, enabling them to effectively navigate the complexities of the market while managing associated risks.

50 Points- You should be always aware of before investing for Cryptocurrency

**1. Conduct Comprehensive Research:** Prior to investing in any Cryptocurrency, dedicate time to thoroughly understand the asset. Investigate the project's objectives, the team behind it, and the underlying technology. A deeper understanding will enhance your investment decisions.

**2. Utilize Trusted Exchanges:** Opt for reputable and established Cryptocurrency exchanges for your trading activities. Well-known platforms typically offer superior security measures and are less prone to fraudulent practices.

**3. Diversify Your Investments:** Avoid concentrating all your funds in a single Cryptocurrency. Distributing your investments across various cryptocurrencies can mitigate risk. If one asset declines, others may still perform favorably.

**4. Safeguard Your Investments:** Ensure the security of your cryptocurrencies by employing strong, unique passwords and activating two-factor authentication. For added protection, consider utilizing a hardware wallet, which keeps your assets offline and secure from potential hackers.

**5. Stay Updated:** Regularly inform yourself about developments in the Cryptocurrency space, including market trends and regulatory changes. This awareness will enable you to make informed investment decisions and adapt your strategy as necessary.

**6. Establish Clear Objectives:** Determine your investment goals regarding cryptocurrencies. Whether you aim for long-term savings or short-term profits, having well-defined objectives will inform your investment approach.

**7. Implement Stop-Loss Orders:** Configure stop-loss orders to automatically liquidate your Cryptocurrency holdings if their price falls to a predetermined level. This strategy can help you minimize losses during market downturns.

**8. Maintain Detailed Records:** Keep a comprehensive log of all your Cryptocurrency transactions, noting the dates of purchase and sale, as well as the prices involved. Effective record-keeping is essential for managing your portfolio and preparing for tax obligations.

**9. Consider Long-Term Investment:** If you have confidence in the future potential of a Cryptocurrency, it may be prudent to hold it for an extended period. This strategy can allow you to capitalize on future growth, despite short-term market volatility.

**10. Understand Tax Responsibilities:** Familiarize yourself with how Cryptocurrency transactions are taxed in your region. It's essential to accurately report your profits and losses to steer clear of complications with tax authorities.

**11. Invest Only What You Can Afford to Lose:** Make sure to invest only the money you can afford to lose when dealing with cryptocurrencies. The market can fluctuate significantly, and there's always a chance of losing your investment.

**12. Use Secure Connections:** Steer clear of accessing your Cryptocurrency accounts over public Wi-Fi or unsecured networks. Opt for a private, secure connection to minimize the risk of your accounts being compromised.

**13. Connect with the Community:** Participate in Cryptocurrency forums, social media groups, or local gatherings to meet other investors. Exchanging knowledge and experiences can offer valuable insights.

**14. Assess Project Fundamentals:** Investigate the essential elements of a Cryptocurrency project, including its purpose, technology, and team. A strong foundation can suggest a higher likelihood of success.

**15. Be Careful with Leverage:** If you're trading with leverage (borrowing funds to trade), proceed with caution. Leverage can amplify both gains and losses, so ensure you fully understand the associated risks.

**16. Regularly Review Your Investment Strategy:** Take the time to periodically evaluate how your investments are performing and whether your strategy needs to be adjusted based on market trends or personal situations.

**17. Use Reputable Wallets:** Keep your Cryptocurrency in trusted wallets that provide robust security features. Hardware wallets are particularly effective for safeguarding your funds against online threats.

**18. Verify ICOs and New Projects:** Before putting your money into Initial Coin Offerings (ICOs) or new cryptocurrencies, ensure the project is legitimate. Look for a comprehensive white paper, a credible team, and a practical use case.

**19. Practice Patience:** Cryptocurrency markets can be quite unpredictable. Avoid making rash decisions based on short-term price fluctuations. Patience can be crucial for achieving long-term gains.

**20. Always Prioritize Security Measures:** Make sure to regularly update your wallet software, utilize antivirus tools, and stay alert for phishing scams. Keeping your security protocols current is essential for safeguarding your assets.

**21. Consider Dollar-Cost Averaging:** Allocate a consistent amount of money to invest in Cryptocurrency at set intervals, no matter the current price. This approach helps to mitigate the effects of market fluctuations by spreading out your investment over time.

**22. Familiarize Yourself with Various Cryptocurrencies:** Take the time to understand the different categories of cryptocurrencies, including coins, tokens, and stablecoins. Each category has unique functions and associated risks.

**23. Seek Expert Guidance:** If you're feeling uncertain about your Cryptocurrency investments or need assistance with your strategy, reach out to a financial advisor who specializes in cryptocurrencies.

**24. Utilize Multi-Signature Wallets:** For enhanced security, opt for multi-signature wallets that require several keys to approve transactions. This adds protection layer against theft.

**25. Monitor Market Trends:** Leverage tools and platforms to keep an eye on market trends and analyze price movements. This data can empower you to make well-informed decisions regarding buying or selling.

**26. Engage in Governance:** If your Cryptocurrency grants you governance rights, make sure to participate in voting and decision-making. Your involvement can shape the future direction of the project.

**27. Stay Alert to Scams:** Always be wary of investment opportunities that claim to offer high returns with minimal risk. Scammers often target those in the Cryptocurrency space, so it's essential to verify any offers and steer clear of anything that seems overly enticing.

**28. Keep Learning:** Continuously educate yourself about the latest trends, technologies, and strategies in the Cryptocurrency realm. Staying updated will help you navigate changes and make informed investment decisions.

**29. Ensure Legal Compliance:** Make sure your Cryptocurrency activities align with local laws and regulations to avoid potential legal complications. This includes following anti-money laundering (AML) and know-your-customer (KYC) guidelines.

**30. Prepare for Market Fluctuations:** Be ready for unexpected declines in Cryptocurrency prices. Having a strategy in place for how to react during market downturns can help safeguard your investments.

**31. Leverage Analytical Tools:** Utilize various analytical tools and platforms to monitor your investments and assess market data. This approach can empower you to make informed, data-driven decisions and keep up with market trends.

**32. Be Aware of Exchange Fees:** Understand the fees associated with trading and transferring cryptocurrencies on exchanges. High fees can eat into your profits, so opt for exchanges that offer competitive rates.

**33. Approach Airdrops with Caution:** While airdrops can provide free tokens, ensure they originate from trustworthy sources. Be vigilant against scams that may use airdrops to collect personal information.

**34. Use Cold Storage for Long-Term Assets:** For investments you plan to hold for an extended period, consider storing your Cryptocurrency in cold storage (offline) to shield it from hacking and online threats.

**35. Review Smart Contract Code:** If you're engaging with decentralized applications (dApps) or smart contracts, take the time to examine their code or seek advice from experts to ensure safety.

**36. Stay Updated on Regulatory Changes:** Keep yourself informed about any shifts in Cryptocurrency regulations, both in your area and worldwide. Changes in regulations can significantly affect the legality and value of your investments.

**37. Understand Your Investment Timeline:** Determine if your investment goals are short-term or long-term, and tailor your strategy to fit. Different timeframes necessitate different tactics.

**38. Perform Regular Security Checks:** Consistently review and enhance your security measures to safeguard your investments against new threats and vulnerabilities.

**39. Rely on Trustworthy News Outlets:** Stay informed about Cryptocurrency news by following credible and established sources to avoid falling for misinformation.

**40. Recognize the Influence of External Factors:** Be mindful that elements like economic trends and global events can influence Cryptocurrency prices and market dynamics.

**41. Practice Responsible Trading:** If you actively trade cryptocurrencies, adopt responsible strategies such as setting trade limits and effectively managing your risks.

**42. Learn About DeFi Risks:** Familiarize yourself with the potential risks associated with decentralized finance (DeFi) platforms, including vulnerabilities in smart contracts and liquidity challenges.

**43. Keep Your Software Current:** Make sure your Cryptocurrency wallet and exchange software are regularly updated with the latest security enhancements and features.

**44. Avoid Making Decisions Based on Emotions:** Base your investment choices on thorough research and a solid strategy instead of emotions like fear or excitement, as emotional decisions can lead to unfavorable results.

**45. Track Project Progress:** Stay updated on the development of the Cryptocurrency projects you invest in. Regular updates and ongoing development are indicators of a robust project.

**46. Make Smart Use of Privacy Features:** If privacy matters to you, opt for cryptocurrencies that provide robust privacy options.

Just remember to stay informed about their limitations and any potential legal concerns.

**47. Assess Market Sentiment:** Keep an eye on how market sentiment and news impact Cryptocurrency prices. By understanding these factors, you can better predict market trends and refine your trading strategy.

**48. Be Cautious with Leverage:** When trading with leverage, steer clear of overextending yourself. High leverage can lead to substantial losses, so it's important to use it judiciously.

**49. Explore Crypto Staking Opportunities:** If available, think about getting involved in staking programs. They can provide extra rewards or income by helping to support the network.

**50. Exercise Patience with New Technologies:** When investing in innovative or emerging technologies, give them time to establish themselves and showcase their true value.

50 Points- Before investment never forget to what you have to do or not to do and don't make haste to invest for Cryptocurrency

**1. Understand Before You Invest:** Make sure you have a solid grasp of Cryptocurrency technology, its purpose, and the associated risks before investing. A lack of understanding can lead to unwise choices.

**2. Stick to Trusted Exchanges:** Only use well-established exchanges with robust security features. Lesser-known platforms may pose a higher risk of fraud or security breaches.

**3. Diversify Your Investments:** Don't put all your funds into a single Cryptocurrency. Spreading your investments across different assets can help safeguard your portfolio against poor performance in one area.

**4. Prioritize Security:** Ignoring security measures can result in the loss of your assets. Always create strong passwords, activate two-factor authentication, and keep your private keys safe.

**5. Avoid Following Trends:** Don't make investment choices based solely on current trends or hype without understanding the underlying fundamentals of the Cryptocurrency. Such decisions can be risky.

**6. Think Independently:** Resist the urge to invest just because others are doing so. Base your decisions on thorough research and your own financial objectives.

**7. Watch for Warning Signs:** Be alert to red flags like promises of guaranteed profits or a lack of transparency. These could signal potential scams or unreliable projects.

**8. Don't Trade Excessively:** Constantly buying and selling cryptocurrencies can lead to higher transaction fees and increased market risk. Limit your trading activities unless you have a clear strategy in place.

**9. Use Secure Connections:** Avoid accessing your Cryptocurrency accounts over public or unsecured networks, as they can be susceptible to hacking. Always opt for secure, private connections.

**10. Invest Wisely:** Only invest what you can afford to lose. Given the volatility of cryptocurrencies, there's always a chance you could lose your entire investment.

**11. Be Mindful of Tax Consequences:** Ignoring the tax responsibilities associated with Cryptocurrency transactions can result in legal complications. Make sure to accurately report your profits and losses in line with tax regulations.

**12. Avoid FOMO (Fear of Missing Out) Driven Investments:** Resist the urge to make investment choices based on the fear of missing out on potential profits. Stick to your research and make thoughtful decisions rather than acting impulsively.

**13. Remember to Secure Your Wallet:** Not backing up your Cryptocurrency wallet and private keys can lead to losing access to your assets. Always keep backups in a secure location.

**14. Steer Clear of Unregulated Ventures:** Exercise caution when considering investments in projects that are not regulated or verified. These types of projects can carry higher risks and may be more susceptible to fraud.

**15. Prioritize Due Diligence:** Always verify the credibility of a Cryptocurrency project before investing. Conduct comprehensive research to steer clear of scams or unreliable opportunities.

**16. Acknowledge Market Fluctuations:** The Cryptocurrency market can experience significant volatility. Be ready for price fluctuations and stay aware of the possibility of sudden value changes.

**17. Be Aware of Smart Contract Risks:** If you're engaging with smart contracts or decentralized applications, understand the potential risks, including coding mistakes or vulnerabilities that could jeopardize your funds.

**18. Watch Out for Pump-and-Dump Schemes:** Stay away from schemes that artificially boost a Cryptocurrency's price for profit. These tactics can result in substantial losses for those who invest late.

**19. Don't Stretch Your Limits:** Avoid taking on too much risk or using excessive leverage, as this can lead to significant losses. Make sure your investments are in line with your risk tolerance and financial situation.

**20. Keep Legal Compliance in Mind:** Ensure that your Cryptocurrency activities comply with local laws and regulations. Failing to do so can result in legal troubles or penalties.

**21. Avoid Unverified Tips:** Steer clear of investment advice from unreliable sources or social media personalities. Always check the information through reputable channels.

**22. Pay Attention to the Project Team:** Investing in cryptocurrencies without understanding the team behind the project can be risky. A trustworthy team is essential for a project's success.

**23. Be Mindful of Privacy Issues:** Understand how your Cryptocurrency transactions could reveal your personal information. Utilize privacy features if necessary, but be aware of their limitations.

**24. Stay Away from Unproven Technology:** Refrain from investing in new technologies or cryptocurrencies that lack a solid track record or clear application. Unproven technologies come with higher risks.

**25. Watch Out for Exchange Fees:** Keep an eye on the fees related to buying, selling, and transferring cryptocurrencies on exchanges. High fees can diminish your investment returns.

**26. Don't Let Emotions Influence Your Choices:** Avoid making investment decisions based on feelings like fear or excitement. Stick to your plan and base your decisions on thorough research.

**27. Keep Up with Project Updates:** Stay informed about the developments of the Cryptocurrency projects you invest in. Regular updates and active progress are positive indicators of a project's health.

**28. Use Secure Storage:** Avoid keeping large amounts of Cryptocurrency in online wallets or exchanges without adequate security. Opt for cold storage for long-term assets.

**29. Steer Clear of Scams:** Do not engage in or support schemes that appear too good to be true or guarantee returns. Scams often target Cryptocurrency investors.

**30. Prioritize Risk Management:** Implement risk management techniques, such as stop-loss orders and diversification, to safeguard your investments from significant losses.

**31. Regularly Review Your Portfolio:** Make it a habit to assess your investment portfolio and strategy frequently to ensure they are in line with your financial goals and current market trends.

**32. Be Aware of Tech Risks:** Stay alert to technological risks such as software glitches or connectivity problems that might impact your Cryptocurrency investments.

**33. Consider Legal Risks:** Keep in mind the potential legal challenges, including adherence to anti-money laundering (AML) and know-your-customer (KYC) regulations.

**34. Avoid High-Risk Trading Strategies:** Steer clear of overly aggressive trading tactics or speculative methods that could result in substantial financial losses.

**35. Verify Project Credibility:** Always check the credibility of a Cryptocurrency project before investing. Look into its white paper, team, and market presence.

**36. Think Long-Term:** Reflect on the long-term potential of your investments rather than just chasing short-term profits. A long-term view can yield greater rewards.

**37. Safeguard Your Personal Information:** Ensure your personal data and private keys are secure. Avoid sharing sensitive information with untrustworthy sources.

**38. Don't Participate in Market Manipulation:** Refrain from engaging in or endorsing activities that manipulate Cryptocurrency prices, as this can damage market integrity and lead to legal repercussions.

**39. Stay Updated on Regulatory Changes:** Keep yourself informed about possible regulatory shifts that could affect your investments and the broader market.

**40. Avoid Following Trends Blindly:** Resist the urge to invest based solely on trends or fads without a solid understanding of the underlying fundamentals of the Cryptocurrency.

**41. Always Be Aware of Scams:** Stay alert for common scams like phishing and fraudulent investment schemes. Make sure to verify the legitimacy of any offers before putting your money in.

**42. Recognize the Influence of Market Sentiment:** It's important to grasp how market sentiment and news can affect Cryptocurrency prices and the behavior of investors.

**43. Evaluate Project Viability:** Before investing, take a close look at whether a Cryptocurrency project has solid technology, market potential, and a competitive advantage.

**44. Stay Updated on Security:** Regularly update your security practices, software, and wallet to safeguard against new threats and vulnerabilities.

**45. Avoid Illegal Activities:** Steer clear of using cryptocurrencies for any illegal transactions. Avoid engaging in such activities because these can lead to serious legal repercussions.

**46. Choose Reliable Exchanges:** Opt for exchanges known for their security and reliability. Avoid those with a history of breaches or operational problems.

**47. Conduct Thorough Research on ICOs:** When investing in Initial Coin Offerings (ICOs), make sure to do your homework. Review the project's white paper, team, and legal standing.

**48. Don't Let Fear Drive Your Decisions:** Base your investment choices on research and strategy rather than fear. Resist the urge to panic sell or buy during market fluctuations.

**49. Be Realistic About Your Knowledge:** Acknowledge your level of understanding regarding cryptocurrencies. If you're unsure, seek advice and further education.

**50. Be Mindful of Market Risks:** Always keep in mind the risks associated with Cryptocurrency investments and be ready for possible negative market conditions.

These practical do's and don'ts provide valuable insights for navigating the Cryptocurrency investment landscape, empowering you to make informed and secure choices.

## Chapter- 5: 50 Safest Ways to Invest in Cryptocurrency

**1. Do Your Own Research (DYOR):** Before diving into any Cryptocurrency investment, take the time to thoroughly investigate the project. Familiarize yourself with its goals, technology, team, and market potential. This will help you make good and safe choices.

**2. Select Trustworthy Exchanges:** Opt for established and trustworthy Cryptocurrency exchanges that prioritize security. Platforms such as Coinbase, Binance, and Kraken are recognized for their dependability.

**3. Activate Two-Factor Authentication (2FA):** Always choose two-factor authentication for the security of your accounts. This adds an additional verification step beyond just your password.

**4. Utilize a Hardware Wallet:** For long-term asset storage, consider using a hardware wallet (like Ledger or Trezor). These devices keep your private keys offline, minimizing the risk of hacking.

**5. Diversify Your Portfolio:** Distribute your investments across various cryptocurrencies instead of concentrating all your funds in one. This strategy helps mitigate the risk of significant losses if one asset underperforms.

**6. Invest Only What You Can Afford to Lose:** Use only the funds you can afford to lose. The Cryptocurrency market can be unpredictable, and there's always a chance of losing your entire investment.

**7. Adhere to Security Best Practices:** Create strong, unique passwords for your accounts and wallets. Steer clear of easily guessable passwords and avoid reusing them across different platforms.

**8. Keep Software Updated:** Regularly update your wallet software and security tools to safeguard against emerging threats and vulnerabilities.

**9. Confirm Project Authenticity:** Before investing in a new Cryptocurrency or project, review its white paper, team, and market presence to verify its legitimacy.

**10. Use Cold Storage for Long-Term Assets:** For long-term investments, opt for cold storage (offline) to shield them from online threats. Cold storage is generally safer than keeping funds on exchanges.

**11. Keep an Eye on Market Trends:** Stay updated on the latest market trends and news. This knowledge allows you to make prompt decisions and adapt your strategy to the current landscape.

**12. Rely on Trusted News Outlets:** Use established and trustworthy news outlets for updates on cryptocurrencies and market changes. Steer clear of rumors and unverified information.

**13. Establish Clear Investment Objectives:** Clarify your investment goals, whether you aim for quick profits or long-term growth. Having specific objectives will help shape your strategy.

**14. Be Aware of Tax Responsibilities:** Familiarize yourself with the tax regulations regarding Cryptocurrency transactions in your area. Properly reporting your gains and losses is crucial to avoid legal complications.

**15. Think About Dollar-Cost Averaging (DCA):** Invest a consistent amount at regular intervals, no matter the price of the Cryptocurrency. This method can help reduce the effects of market fluctuations.

**16. Choose Secure Wallets:** Opt for wallets that are known for their strong security measures and positive reputations. Look for features like encryption and backup options.

**17. Verify Regulatory Compliance:** Make sure that the exchanges and projects you invest in adhere to local regulations. This can help you avoid legal issues and create a safer investment environment.

**18. Don't Invest Based on Hype:** Avoid making investment choices driven by excitement or fear of missing out. Stick to your research and refrain from impulsive decisions.

**19. Engage with Project Communities:** Become a part of the community surrounding any Cryptocurrency project that interests you. Interacting with other users and developers can offer valuable perspectives.

**20. Implement Stop-Loss Orders:** Use stop-loss orders to automatically sell your Cryptocurrency if its price falls below a specified threshold. This strategy will help you decrease potential losses.

**21. Stay Alert for Phishing Scams:** Always be cautious of emails or messages that request your private keys or login details. It's essential to verify the sender before clicking on any links or sharing sensitive information.

**22. Review Project White Papers:** Take the time to read the white papers of Cryptocurrency projects carefully. They contain comprehensive details about the project's objectives, technology, and practical applications.

**23. Assess the Team Behind Projects:** Investigate the background and reputation of the team involved in a Cryptocurrency project. A trustworthy and experienced team is vital for the project's success.

**24. Engage in Governance When Possible:** If the Cryptocurrency offers community voting or governance options, get involved in these processes to help shape the project's future.

**25. Utilize Multi-Signature Wallets:** For enhanced security, opt for multi-signature wallets that require several approvals to finalize transactions. This will protect you against unauthorized access.

**26. Avoid High-Risk Trading:** Stay away from highly speculative trading tactics or excessive leverage. These approaches can result in significant financial losses.

**27. Verify Exchange Security Protocols:** Make sure the exchange you choose has strong security measures in place, such as encryption, regular security audits, and insurance against hacking incidents.

**28. Steer Clear of Pump-and-Dump Schemes:** Be cautious of schemes that artificially boost a Cryptocurrency's price to lure in investors. These tactics can lead to considerable financial losses.

**29. Choose Reliable Staking Services:** If you decide to stake your assets, select reputable and well-reviewed services to ensure your staked assets are managed safely.

**30. Be Aware of Fees:** Familiarize yourself with the fees related to trading, transferring, and holding cryptocurrencies. High fees can affect your overall returns, so opt for services with fair pricing.

**31. Exercise Patience with Your Investments:** The Cryptocurrency market can experience significant fluctuations. It's important to refrain from making hasty decisions based on temporary price changes and to remain patient with your investment choices.

**32. Regularly Evaluate Your Portfolio:** Take the time to periodically review your investment portfolio to ensure it meets your financial goals and risk appetite. Make adjustments to your holdings as necessary.

**33. Be Wary of Unverified ICOs:** Approach Initial Coin Offerings (ICOs) with caution, especially those that lack transparency or credibility. Always verify the legitimacy of a project before investing your money.

**34. Look for Security Audits:** For decentralized finance (DeFi) projects or smart contracts, check if they have been subjected to security audits. Because these audits are very important for identifying and mitigating potential vulnerabilities.

**35. Use Encrypted Communication:** When discussing Cryptocurrency investments or sharing sensitive information, opt for encrypted communication methods to safeguard your privacy.

**36. Avoid Public Wi-Fi for Transactions:** Steer clear of accessing your Cryptocurrency accounts over public Wi-Fi networks. Always use a secure, private connection to protect your sensitive information.

**37. Be Careful with Airdrops:** If you decide to participate in airdrops, make sure they originate from trustworthy sources. Be cautious of airdrops that request personal information or appear suspicious.

**38. Grasp Cryptocurrency Volatility:** Understand that Cryptocurrency prices can vary dramatically. Be ready for fluctuations and avoid making impulsive decisions based on price changes.

**39. Seek Professional Guidance:** If you're uncertain about your investment strategy or need assistance, consider consulting a financial advisor who specializes in Cryptocurrency investments.

**40. Choose Secure Exchanges for Transactions:** When buying or selling cryptocurrencies, opt for exchanges that are recognized for their robust security measures and excellent customer support.

**41. Limit Exposure to Individual Assets:** It's wise not to put too much of your portfolio into one Cryptocurrency. Diversifying your investments can help mitigate risks and shield you from significant losses.

**42. Keep an Eye on Regulatory Updates:** Make sure to stay informed about any regulatory changes that might impact your investments. Be ready to adjust your strategy to align with new regulations.

**43. Familiarize Yourself with Project Roadmaps:** Take the time to examine the roadmap of any Cryptocurrency project to grasp its future objectives and plans. A well-defined roadmap can signal a project's likelihood of success.

**44. Be Cautious of Unsolicited Investment Proposals:** Steer clear of investment opportunities that come your way unexpectedly. Always verify their credibility before considering any financial commitment.

**45. Choose Reliable Trading Platforms:** When engaging in active trading, opt for platforms that have positive reviews and a solid reputation. Avoid those known for security breaches or inadequate customer service.

**46. Think About Using Trusted Asset Managers:** If you prefer a more hands-off investment style, consider working with Cryptocurrency asset managers who have a strong reputation for effectively managing and safeguarding investments.

**47. Learn About Various Investment Options:** Educate yourself on the different ways to invest in cryptocurrencies, including direct purchases, futures, ETFs, and index funds, to determine what aligns best with your goals.

**48. Stay Alert for Project Scams:** Be cautious of projects that promise unrealistic returns or lack clear information. Scammers often attract investors with exaggerated claims.

**49. Keep Up with Technological Advances:** Stay updated on developments in blockchain technology and Cryptocurrency innovations to make well-informed investment choices.

**50. Maintain Good Cybersecurity Practices:** Regularly check your devices for malware, use antivirus software, and be careful with your online activities to safeguard your investments from cyber threats.

By adhering to these prudent investment strategies, you can better protect your Cryptocurrency holdings and navigate the market with increased assurance.

# Major Markets and Platforms to Invest

Chapter- 6: Some of the major markets and platforms where you can invest in Cryptocurrencies:

## 1. Cryptocurrency Exchanges

**Centralized Exchanges (CEXs):** These are online platforms that act as intermediaries between buyers and sellers of cryptocurrencies. They provide a user-friendly interface and often have high liquidity.
**Binance:** One of the largest exchanges globally, known for its extensive list of cryptocurrencies and high trading volume.
**Coinbase:** A popular exchange in the U.S. known for its ease of use and regulatory compliance.
**Kraken:** Offers a wide range of cryptocurrencies and is known for its strong security measures.
**Bitfinex:** Known for its advanced trading features and high liquidity.
**Bittrex:** Offers a large selection of cryptocurrencies and is known for its security.
**Decentralized Exchanges (DEXs):** These operate without a central authority and allow peer-to-peer trading of cryptocurrencies.
**Uniswap:** A decentralized exchange that operates on the Ethereum blockchain, allowing users to trade ERC-20 tokens.

**SushiSwap:** A fork of Uniswap with additional features and community governance.
**PancakeSwap:** Operates on the Binance Smart Chain (BSC) and offers lower fees compared to Ethereum-based DEXs.

## 2. Cryptocurrency Trading Platforms

**Brokerages:** Platforms that allow you to buy and sell cryptocurrencies directly, often with simpler interfaces than exchanges.
**eToro:** A social trading platform that offers Cryptocurrency trading alongside other assets like stocks and forex.
**Robinhood:** Known for commission-free trading of various assets, including cryptocurrencies.
**Gemini:** A U.S.-based brokerage with strong regulatory compliance and user-friendly features.

## 3. Cryptocurrency Investment Funds

**Exchange-Traded Funds (ETFs):** These are investment funds traded on stock exchanges, similar to stocks, but they track the performance of a Cryptocurrency or a basket of cryptocurrencies.
**ProShares Bitcoin Strategy ETF:** Offers exposure to Bitcoin futures contracts.
**Purpose Bitcoin ETF:** Provides direct exposure to Bitcoin and is available on the Toronto Stock Exchange (TSX).
**Grayscale Bitcoin Trust (GBTC):** Allows investors to gain exposure to Bitcoin through a traditional brokerage account.
**Crypto Index Funds:** These funds invest in a diversified basket of cryptocurrencies, aiming to mirror the performance of a Cryptocurrency index.
**Bitwise 10 Crypto Index Fund:** Tracks the performance of the top 10 cryptocurrencies by market cap.
**Coinbase Index Fund:** Aims to provide diversified exposure to a broad range of cryptocurrencies available on Coinbase.

## 4. Cryptocurrency Staking Platforms

**Staking Platforms:** Platforms where you can stake certain cryptocurrencies to earn rewards or interest.
**Binance Staking:** Allows users to stake various cryptocurrencies and earn rewards.
**Kraken Staking:** Offers staking for multiple cryptocurrencies with competitive rewards.
**Coinbase Earn:** Provides opportunities to earn rewards by staking supported cryptocurrencies.

## 5. Cryptocurrency Mining

**Mining Pools:** Groups of miners who combine their computational resources to increase the chances of successfully mining a block and share the rewards.
**Slush Pool:** One of the oldest mining pools, supporting Bitcoin and other cryptocurrencies.
**F2Pool:** A major mining pool with support for multiple cryptocurrencies, including Bitcoin and Ethereum.
**Antpool:** Operated by Bitmain, offering mining services for various cryptocurrencies.
**Cloud Mining Services:** Platforms that allow you to rent mining power without owning the hardware.
**Genesis Mining:** Offers cloud mining contracts for various cryptocurrencies.
**Hashflare:** Provides cloud mining services for Bitcoin and other digital currencies.

## 6. Cryptocurrency Savings Accounts

**Crypto Savings Accounts:** Platforms that offer interest on deposited cryptocurrencies, similar to traditional savings accounts.
**BlockFi:** Provides interest-bearing accounts for Bitcoin, Ethereum, and other cryptocurrencies.

**Celsius Network:** Offers competitive interest rates on a variety of cryptocurrencies.
**Nexo:** Provides interest on Cryptocurrency deposits and instant crypto-backed loans.

## 7. Initial Coin Offerings (ICOs) and Token Sales

**ICO Platforms:** These platforms host initial coin offerings where new cryptocurrencies are sold to investors.
**CoinList:** Hosts ICOs and token sales for new and established projects.
**Binance Launchpad:** Binance's platform for new Cryptocurrency projects to raise funds through token sales.

## 8. Decentralized Finance (DeFi) Platforms

**DeFi Platforms:** These offer financial services such as lending, borrowing, and trading without traditional intermediaries.
**Compound:** A decentralized lending protocol where users can lend and borrow cryptocurrencies.
**Aave:** Offers decentralized lending and borrowing with various cryptocurrencies and stablecoins.
**MakerDAO:** Provides decentralized stablecoin issuance and lending services.

## 9. Cryptocurrency Wallets

**Hot Wallets:** Online wallets that are connected to the internet, allowing for easy access to your cryptocurrencies.
**MetaMask:** A popular browser extension and mobile wallet for Ethereum-based tokens.
**Trust Wallet:** A mobile wallet supporting multiple cryptocurrencies, including Ethereum and Binance Smart Chain tokens.
**Cold Wallets:** Offline wallets that provide enhanced security by storing private keys offline.

**Ledger Nano X:** A hardware wallet with Bluetooth connectivity for ease of use.
**Trezor Model T:** A hardware wallet with a touch screen and support for a wide range of cryptocurrencies.

## 10. Cryptocurrency Payment Platforms

**Payment Platforms:** Services that allow businesses and individuals to accept and make payments using cryptocurrencies.
**BitPay:** Provides payment processing solutions for businesses and individuals using Bitcoin and Bitcoin Cash.
**CoinGate:** Offers Cryptocurrency payment gateway services for businesses and integration with various cryptocurrencies.
These markets and platforms provide various ways to invest in and engage with cryptocurrencies, each with its own set of features, benefits, and risks.

Chapter- 7: Although no investment is completely devoid of risk, certain cryptocurrencies are typically regarded as safer options due to their well-established reputations, significant market presence, and robust development teams. Below is a compilation of 25 widely recognized cryptocurrencies that are frequently perceived as relatively safer investments, accompanied by reasons for their stability.

### 1. Bitcoin- (BTC)
**Overview:** The original and most recognized Cryptocurrency, often dubbed "digital gold."
**Reason for Stability:** It boasts the largest market cap, is widely accepted, and benefits from a robust network effect.

### 2. Ethereum- (ETH)
**Overview:** A decentralized platform that supports smart contracts and decentralized applications (DApps).
**Reason for Stability:** It ranks second in market capitalization, has a vast developer community, and is undergoing significant upgrades with Ethereum 2.0.

### 3. Binance Coin- (BNB)
**Overview:** The official coin of the Binance Exchange, utilized for trading fee payments and token sales.

**Reason for Stability:** It enjoys strong support from Binance, one of the largest exchanges, and has a growing range of applications within its ecosystem.

## 4. Cardano- (ADA)
**Overview:** A blockchain platform that emphasizes sustainability and scalability, driven by research.
**Reason for Stability:** It is supported by academic research and a dedicated development team, with a vision for long-term success.

## 5. Solana- (SOL)
**Overview:** A high-speed blockchain built for efficient and scalable decentralized applications.
**Reason for Stability:** It is recognized for its rapid transaction speeds and low costs, along with increasing adoption and solid technology.

## 6. Polkadot- (DOT)
**Overview:** A multi-chain platform that allows various blockchains to work together and share data.
**Reason for Stability:** It is led by Dr. Gavin Wood, an Ethereum co-founder, and emphasizes interoperability and scalability.

## 7. Ripple- (XRP)
**Overview:** A digital payment protocol designed to streamline cross-border transactions.
**Reason for Stability:** It has established strong partnerships with financial institutions and focuses on addressing real-world payment challenges.

## 8. Chainlink- (LINK)
**Overview:** A decentralized oracle network that links smart contracts to real-world data.
**Reason for Stability:** It plays a crucial role in many DeFi applications, supported by strong partnerships and integration with major projects.

## 9. Litecoin- (LTC)
**Overview:** Commonly known as the "silver" to Bitcoin's "gold," it was created to offer a quicker alternative to Bitcoin.
**Reason for Stability:** It has a proven history, emphasizing speedy and cost-effective transactions.

## 10. USD Coin- (USDC)
**Overview:** This stablecoin is tied to the U.S. dollar, ensuring both stability and liquidity.
**Reason for Stability:** It is fully backed by USD reserves on a 1:1 basis, with regular audits for transparency.

## 11. Stellar- (XLM)
**Overview:** A platform designed to enhance cross-border payments and promote financial inclusion.
**Reason for Stability:** It prioritizes partnerships with financial institutions and is dedicated to fostering financial inclusion.

## 12. Uniswap- (UNI)
**Overview:** A top decentralized exchange (DEX) that enables users to trade ERC-20 tokens.
**Reason for Stability:** As a key player in the DeFi sector, it boasts high trading volumes and substantial liquidity.

## 13. Aave- (AAVE)
**Overview:** A decentralized platform for lending and borrowing within the DeFi ecosystem.
**Reason for Stability:** It has a well-established reputation in the DeFi space, supported by a robust platform and ongoing development.

## 14. VeChain- (VET)
**Overview:** A blockchain solution aimed at enhancing supply chain management and enterprise applications.

**Reason for Stability:** It has formed strong partnerships with major corporations and focuses on practical use cases.

## 15. Cosmos- (ATOM)
**Overview:** A network of interconnected blockchains designed to address scalability and interoperability challenges.
**Reason for Stability:** It offers an innovative solution for blockchain interoperability and has a vibrant development community.

## 16. Algorand- (ALGO)
**Overview:** A high-performance blockchain built for rapid transactions and smart contracts.
**Reason for Stability:** It emphasizes scalability and efficiency, backed by a strong team and increasing adoption.

## 17. Terra- (LUNA)
**Overview:** A blockchain platform centered around stablecoins and financial applications.
**Reason for Stability:** It is experiencing growth in DeFi and stablecoin usage, supported by a robust ecosystem of applications.

## 18. Internet Computer- (ICP)
**Overview:** A blockchain built to support smart contracts and decentralized applications at lightning speed.
**Reason for Stability:** Supported by the DFINITY Foundation, it aims to revolutionize the decentralization of the web.

## 19. Filecoin- (FIL)
**Overview:** A decentralized storage network enabling users to lease out their unused storage capacity.
**Reason for Stability:** It meets a genuine demand for decentralized storage solutions, with increasing interest in its technology.

## 20. Tezos- (XTZ)
**Overview:** A blockchain platform that emphasizes self-amending protocols and governance on the blockchain.
**Reason for Stability:** Renowned for its governance structure and capability to upgrade seamlessly without hard forks.

## 21. Zcash- (ZEC)
**Overview:** A Cryptocurrency that prioritizes privacy, offering shielded transactions.
**Reason for Stability:** It delivers privacy features while ensuring a strong commitment to security and transparency.

## 22. Dash- (DASH)
**Overview:** A Cryptocurrency designed for quick and anonymous transactions.
**Reason for Stability:** Recognized for its speed and privacy capabilities, backed by a robust development team and an engaged community.

## 23. Monero- (XMR)
**Overview:** A Cryptocurrency focused on privacy, providing confidential and untraceable transactions.
**Reason for Stability:** It places a strong emphasis on privacy and fungibility, with continuous development aimed at enhancing security.

## 24. SushiSwap- (SUSHI)
**Overview:** A decentralized exchange and automated market maker (AMM) platform.
**Reason for Stability:** A derivative of Uniswap that offers additional features and enjoys strong community backing.

## 25. Maker- (MKR)
**Overview:** A governance token for MakerDAO, which manages the DAI stablecoin.

**Reason for Stability:** It plays a crucial role in the DeFi ecosystem, focusing on stablecoin issuance and decentralized governance.

These cryptocurrencies are well-regarded and have made their mark in the crypto landscape. However, it's important to keep in mind that all investments come with risks, so thorough research and consideration of your risk tolerance are essential before making any investment decisions.

Chapter- 8: Investing in Cryptocurrency can be exciting and potentially profitable, but it comes with several risks. Here's a breakdown of the main risk factors involved, explained in simple and human-friendly terms:

## 1. Market Fluctuations
**Explanation:** The prices of cryptocurrencies can fluctuate wildly in a very short time. For instance, a coin valued at $100 today could plummet to $50 or soar to $200 within just a week.
**Impact:** This volatility can create opportunities for significant profits, but it also poses the risk of considerable losses. Such unpredictable swings can be quite stressful for investors.

## 2. Strategic Regulatory Ambiguity
**Explanation:** Governments globally are still determining how to approach Cryptocurrency regulation. New laws or guidelines can affect the value or legality of specific cryptocurrencies.
**Impact:** Shifts in regulations can trigger abrupt price declines or even render certain cryptocurrencies illegal in various regions.

## 3. Security Vulnerabilities
**Explanation:** Cryptocurrencies are kept in digital wallets, which can be susceptible to hacking or theft. Cybercriminals often target exchanges and wallets.

**Impact:** If your wallet or exchange account is compromised, you risk losing your entire investment. It's essential to choose secure platforms and adhere to best security practices.

## 4. Absence of Consumer Safeguards
**Explanation:** Unlike conventional banks or financial institutions, cryptocurrencies typically lack consumer protections. If issues arise, there may be limited options for recourse.
**Impact:** Losing access to your wallet or falling prey to a scam can make it extremely challenging, if not impossible, to recover your funds.

## 5. Scams and Deception
**Explanation:** The Cryptocurrency landscape is filled with scams, including Ponzi schemes, fraudulent ICOs (Initial Coin Offerings), and phishing scams.
**Impact:** You could be misled into investing in bogus projects or lose money to scammers posing as legitimate businesses.

## 6. Knowledge Gaps
**Explanation:** The technology behind cryptocurrencies and the market itself can be intricate and perplexing. Misunderstanding their workings can lead to poor investment choices.
**Impact:** Without a solid grasp of the concepts, you might make uninformed decisions that could lead to financial losses.

## 7. Liquidity Challenges
**Explanation:** Certain cryptocurrencies experience low trading activity or lack widespread acceptance, making it difficult to buy or sell them quickly without impacting their price.
**Impact:** If you find yourself needing to sell your investment in a hurry, you may struggle to secure a favorable price or even locate potential buyers.

## 8. Technological Vulnerabilities

**Explanation:** Cryptocurrencies depend on technology such as blockchain, which can be prone to bugs, security flaws, or software malfunctions that may hinder their functionality.

**Impact:** Technical difficulties can result in financial losses or interruptions in service. It's wise to invest in projects that prioritize robust development and security protocols to reduce this risk.

## 9. Influence of Market

**Explanation:** The Cryptocurrency market can be influenced by large investors, often referred to as "whales," who can sway prices through significant trades.

**Impact:** Such manipulation can cause erratic price fluctuations, complicating your ability to make well-informed investment choices.

## 10. Project Sustainability

**Explanation:** Not all Cryptocurrency projects will thrive or fulfill their promises. They may falter due to insufficient adoption, technical challenges, or management failures.

**Impact:** Investing in these projects could lead to financial losses if they fail or experience a substantial drop in value.

## 11. Legal and Regulatory Challenges

**Explanation:** The legal landscape for cryptocurrencies varies greatly across different countries and is continually changing. Some nations may impose restrictions or outright bans.

**Impact:** Shifts in the legal status of cryptocurrencies, whether locally or globally, can affect their value and your capacity to trade or utilize them.

## 12. Counterparty Risks

**Explanation:** When engaging with exchanges, wallets, or decentralized finance (DeFi) platforms, you depend on third parties to manage your assets, which could fail or act unethically.

**Impact:** If a platform faces bankruptcy, gets hacked, or commits fraud, you risk losing your investments.

## 13. Uncertain Long-Term Value
**Explanation:** The future worth of many cryptocurrencies remains unpredictable. While some may succeed, others could fade away.
**Impact:** There's no assurance that a Cryptocurrency will maintain its value over time, which might result in losses if it becomes irrelevant or collapses.

## 14. Emotional Investing
**Explanation:** The thrill or anxiety of missing out (FOMO) can drive investors to make hasty choices based on feelings instead of facts.
**Impact:** Decisions made on emotion can lead to buying at high prices and selling at low ones, resulting in financial losses.

## 15. Difficulty in Valuation
**Explanation:** Figuring out the true value of a Cryptocurrency can be tough due to the absence of conventional financial indicators and the speculative nature of the market.
**Impact:** Without clear methods for valuation, it's challenging to determine if a Cryptocurrency is overpriced or undervalued.

## 16. Technological Dependencies
**Explanation:** Cryptocurrencies rely on their underlying technology, like blockchain. Any issues with this technology can impact the Cryptocurrency's performance.
**Impact:** Technical problems can cause operational difficulties or influence the Cryptocurrency's market value.

## 17. Environmental Concerns
**Explanation:** Certain cryptocurrencies, especially Bitcoin, consume significant energy for mining, raising environmental issues that could prompt regulatory changes.

**Impact:** Environmental regulations might influence the value or legality of cryptocurrencies that require high energy consumption.

## 18. Geopolitical Risks
**Explanation:** Political unrest or conflicts can impact Cryptocurrency markets. Shifts in international relations or trade policies can affect Cryptocurrency values.
**Impact:** Geopolitical developments can create market fluctuations and influence the worth of your investments.

## 19. Insufficient Institutional Backing
**Explanation:** Although there is an increase in institutional investment in cryptocurrencies, not every institution is participating. The absence of institutional backing can influence market stability.
**Impact:** A lack of institutional engagement may lead to reduced market liquidity and increased volatility.

## 20. Challenges in Grasping Tax Responsibilities
**Explanation:** Cryptocurrency tax regulations can be intricate and differ from one country to another. Misinterpreting or neglecting tax obligations can result in penalties.
**Impact:** Failing to accurately report Cryptocurrency transactions may lead to legal complications or unforeseen tax burdens.

## 21. Narrow Range of Applications
**Explanation:** Not every Cryptocurrency has practical or widely accepted applications. A deficiency in real-world usage can impact their value.
**Impact:** Cryptocurrencies with limited applications might find it difficult to sustain their value or gain popularity in the market.

## 22. Scam Projects
**Explanation:** Some initiatives within the Cryptocurrency realm are created to deceive investors. This includes fraudulent ICOs or scam tokens.

**Impact:** Putting money into scam projects can lead to a complete loss of investment.

## 23. Shifts in Regulations in Key Markets
**Explanation:** Alterations in regulations within major markets (such as the U.S. or China) can significantly affect Cryptocurrency values.
**Impact:** Abrupt regulatory shifts can cause sharp price changes or disrupt the market.

## 24. Insufficient Research
**Explanation:** Investing without comprehensive research can result in poor investment decisions. Lacking an understanding of a Cryptocurrency's fundamentals can be risky.
**Impact:** Insufficient research may lead to investments in projects that are overvalued or have underlying issues.

## 25. Network Failures
**Explanation:** Cryptocurrencies rely heavily on their blockchain networks. Any failures or complications within these networks can hinder transactions or overall operations.
**Impact:** Issues with the network can significantly impact both the performance and value of a Cryptocurrency.

By being aware of these risks, you can make smarter choices and manage your Cryptocurrency investments more effectively. It's essential to approach Cryptocurrency investing with care and comprehensive research.

# Who can Invest?

Chapter- 9: Investing in Cryptocurrency is open to a broad range of individuals and entities, but there are some important considerations and requirements based on personal circumstances and regulatory environments. Here's a detailed look at "Who can invest in Cryptocurrency":

## 1. Individual Investors
**Description:** People who want to invest their personal funds in cryptocurrencies.
**Considerations:**
Age: Most platforms require investors to be at least 18 years old.
KYC/AML: Know Your Customer (KYC) and AntiMoney Laundering (AML) regulations often require providing personal identification and proof of address.
Financial Situation: Individuals should assess their financial situation and risk tolerance before investing, as Cryptocurrency investments can be highly volatile.

## 2. Institutional Investors
**Description:** Organizations such as hedge funds, mutual funds, and venture capital firms that invest on behalf of their clients or shareholders.
**Considerations:**

Regulatory Compliance: Institutional investors often have to comply with strict regulatory requirements and may have more sophisticated strategies and risk management practices.
Investment Strategies: They may invest in cryptocurrencies directly, through funds, or by investing in companies involved in the crypto space.

### 3. Accredited or Sophisticated Investors
**Description:** Individuals or entities that meet specific financial criteria set by regulatory bodies, often involving a high net worth or significant income.
**Considerations:**
Financial Criteria: In the U.S., an accredited investor typically has a net worth of over $1 million (excluding primary residence) or earns over $200,000 annually ($300,000 with a spouse).
Access to Opportunities: Accredited investors may have access to investment opportunities that are not available to the general public, such as certain ICOs (Initial Coin Offerings) or private placements.

### 4. Retail Investors
**Description:** Individual investors who invest in smaller amounts and typically use online exchanges or trading platforms.
**Considerations:**
Ease of Access: Retail investors can easily access cryptocurrencies through various exchanges and wallets.
Regulations: They need to be aware of and comply with local regulations and tax implications.

### 5. Companies or Corporate Investors
**Description:** Companies and corporations that invest in cryptocurrencies as part of their business strategy or treasury management.
**Considerations:**
Corporate Policy: Companies must consider their investment policy, risk management practices, and regulatory compliance.

Tax and Accounting: Corporate investors need to handle complex tax and accounting issues related to Cryptocurrency investments.

## 6. Nonprofit Organizations
**Description:** Charities and other nonprofit entities that may invest in cryptocurrencies to diversify their asset base or to accept donations in crypto form.
**Considerations:**
Governance: Nonprofits must follow their governance policies and ensure that any investment aligns with their mission and financial strategy.
Regulatory Compliance: They must adhere to regulations and reporting requirements specific to their jurisdiction.

## 7. Individual Professional Traders
**Description:** Individuals or entities that engage in trading cryptocurrencies as a primary business or occupation.
**Considerations:**
Expertise: Professional traders typically have extensive knowledge and experience in market analysis and trading strategies.
Tools and Resources: They often use advanced tools and platforms for trading and risk management.

## 8. Blockchain and Crypto Enthusiasts
**Description:** Individuals who have a personal interest in blockchain technology and cryptocurrencies and may invest as a hobby or passion.
**Considerations:**
Education: Enthusiasts should educate themselves about the technology, market dynamics, and risks involved.
Investment Approach: They might invest in specific projects or tokens based on their interests or beliefs about the technology's potential.

## 9. EarlyStage Investors
**Description:** Investors who are willing to invest in new and emerging cryptocurrencies or blockchain projects at an early stage.
**Considerations:**
High Risk: Earlystage investments can be highly speculative and risky, as many new projects fail.
Due Diligence: Thorough research and due diligence are essential to assess the viability and potential of earlystage investments.

## 10. Governments and Sovereign Wealth Funds
**Description:** National governments or sovereign wealth funds that invest in cryptocurrencies as part of their financial strategy.
**Considerations:**
Strategic Goals: These entities might invest to diversify their holdings, support innovation, or explore potential applications of blockchain technology.
Regulatory Framework: They need to adhere to complex regulatory and legal frameworks.

## 10. Regulatory and laws
**Considerations:**
Legal Restrictions: Some countries have restrictions or bans on Cryptocurrency investments. It's important to be aware of and comply with local laws and regulations regarding Cryptocurrency.
Tax Implications: Different jurisdictions have varying tax rules for Cryptocurrency transactions. It is not easy to understand and complying with these tax obligations.

## Conclusion
In summary, almost anyone with access to Cryptocurrency exchanges and the ability to meet regulatory requirements can invest in cryptocurrencies. However, it's crucial to understand the risks, conduct thorough research, and ensure compliance with local regulations before investing.

# Full Form and Abbreviation used in Cryptocurrency

**Chapter- 10: Full form and definition of each abbreviation used in the Cryptocurrency space:**

General Terms

### ADA- Cardano
**Definition:** A blockchain platform focused on security, scalability, and sustainability, designed for smart contracts and decentralized applications (DApps).

### BTC- Bitcoin
**Definition:** The first and most well-known Cryptocurrency, often referred to as "digital gold," created by an anonymous person or group known as Satoshi Nakamoto.

### ETH- Ethereum
**Definition:** A blockchain platform that enables the creation and execution of smart contracts and decentralized applications (DApps) on its network.

### LTC- Litecoin
**Definition:** A peer-to-peer Cryptocurrency created as a lighter, faster alternative to Bitcoin, known for quicker transaction times.

**XRP- Ripple**
**Definition:** A digital payment protocol and Cryptocurrency designed for fast, low-cost international money transfers.

**XMR- Monero**
**Definition:** A privacy-focused Cryptocurrency that emphasizes confidentiality and untraceability in transactions.

**DASH- Digital Cash**
**Definition:** A Cryptocurrency aimed at providing fast, anonymous transactions, with features such as PrivateSend and InstantSend.

**USDT- Tether (US Dollar Tether)**
**Definition:** A stablecoin pegged to the U.S. dollar, used to provide stability and liquidity within the Cryptocurrency market.

**USDC- USD Coin**
**Definition:** A stablecoin pegged to the U.S. dollar, backed by reserves and regularly audited to ensure its value remains stable.

## Technical Terms

**ALT- Alternative Coin**
**Definition:** Any Cryptocurrency other than Bitcoin, often referred to as altcoins.

**API- Application Programming Interface**
**Definition:** A set of rules and tools for building software applications, allowing different programs to communicate with each other.

**ASIC- Application-Specific Integrated Circuit**
**Definition:** A type of hardware specifically designed to perform a particular task, such as mining a specific Cryptocurrency.

## BIP- Bitcoin Improvement Proposal
**Definition:** A formal proposal for improvements to the Bitcoin protocol, which includes changes and enhancements to Bitcoin's technology.

## CEX- Centralized Exchange
**Definition:** A Cryptocurrency exchange operated by a central authority, where users trade cryptocurrencies in a managed environment.

## Dapp- Decentralized Application
**Definition:** An application that runs on a decentralized network, such as a blockchain, rather than a central server.

## DEX- Decentralized Exchange
**Definition:** A Cryptocurrency exchange that operates without a central authority, allowing users to trade directly with each other.

## ERC- Ethereum Request for Comments
**Definition:** A process for proposing and discussing standards for the Ethereum blockchain.

## ERC-20- Ethereum Request for Comments - 20
**Definition:** A standard for creating fungible tokens on the Ethereum blockchain, which allows for interoperability between different tokens.

## ERC-721- Ethereum Request for Comments - 721
**Definition:** A standard for creating non-fungible tokens (NFTs) on the Ethereum blockchain, allowing for unique and indivisible tokens.

## FOMO- Fear of Missing Out
**Definition:** An emotional response where investors worry about missing out on potential gains, often leading to impulsive decisions.

## FUD- Fear, Uncertainty, and Doubt
**Definition:** A strategy used to spread negative information or rumors to create fear and uncertainty, often to manipulate market behavior.

## GUI- Graphical User Interface
**Definition:** A user interface that allows users to interact with software through graphical elements like icons and buttons, rather than text commands.

## HODL- Hold On for Dear Life
**Definition:** A misspelling of "hold" that has come to represent a strategy of keeping Cryptocurrency investments regardless of market fluctuations.

## ICO- Initial Coin Offering
**Definition:** A fundraising method where new cryptocurrencies are sold to investors in exchange for established cryptocurrencies or fiat money.

## IEO- Initial Exchange Offering
**Definition:** A type of fundraising event where a new Cryptocurrency is offered to investors through a Cryptocurrency exchange platform.

## IFO- Initial Farm Offering
**Definition:** A fundraising method used in the DeFi space where new tokens are distributed in exchange for liquidity or staking in a decentralized exchange.

## KYC- Know Your Customer
**Definition:** A process used by financial institutions and exchanges to verify the identity of their customers to prevent fraud and comply with regulations.

## LTC- Litecoin
**Definition:** A Cryptocurrency created as a faster and lighter alternative to Bitcoin, known for its quicker transaction confirmation times.

## MVP- Minimum Viable Product
**Definition:** The most basic version of a product that is still functional and can be released to users to test its viability and gather feedback.

## NFT- Non-Fungible Token
**Definition:** A unique digital asset that represents ownership of a specific item or piece of content, typically used for digital art, collectibles, and other unique assets.

## PoW- Proof of Work
**Definition:** A consensus mechanism where miners solve complex mathematical problems to validate transactions and create new blocks on the blockchain.

## PoS- Proof of Stake
**Definition:** A consensus mechanism where validators are chosen to create new blocks and validate transactions based on the number of coins they hold and are willing to "stake" as collateral.

## RPC- Remote Procedure Call
**Definition:** A protocol that allows a program to execute code or retrieve data from a server over a network.

## SHA- Secure Hash Algorithm
**Definition:** A family of cryptographic hash functions used for securing data by producing a fixed-size hash value from input data.

**SMA- Simple Moving Average**
**Definition:** A statistical calculation used to analyze data points by creating a series of averages over a specific period, commonly used in financial markets.

**TPS- Transactions Per Second**
**Definition:** A measure of how many transactions a blockchain or Cryptocurrency network can process within one second.

**TVL- Total Value Locked**
**Definition:** The total amount of assets locked in a decentralized finance (DeFi) protocol, often used to measure its popularity and usage.

**UTXO- Unspent Transaction Output**
**Definition:** The amount of Cryptocurrency that remains after a transaction, which can be used in future transactions as input.

## Cryptocurrency Exchanges and Wallets

**Binance- Binance Coin (BNB)**
**Definition:** The native Cryptocurrency of the Binance exchange, used for paying trading fees and participating in token sales.

**Coinbase- Coinbase Pro**
**Definition:** The professional trading platform of Coinbase, offering advanced trading features and tools.

**Kraken- Kraken Exchange**
**Definition:** A popular Cryptocurrency exchange known for its robust security and wide range of supported cryptocurrencies.

**Bitfinex- Bitfinex Exchange**
**Definition:** A Cryptocurrency exchange known for its advanced trading features and high liquidity.

### Bittrex- Bittrex Exchange
**Definition:** A Cryptocurrency exchange offering a wide selection of digital assets and trading pairs.

## Investment and Financial Terms

### APY- Annual Percentage Yield
**Definition:** The rate of return on an investment over one year, taking into account compound interest.

### APR- Annual Percentage Rate
**Definition:** The annual rate charged for borrowing or earned through an investment, excluding compound interest.

### CAP- Market Capitalization
**Definition:** The total value of a Cryptocurrency, calculated by multiplying its current price by the total number of coins in circulation.

### ROI- Return on Investment
**Definition:** A measure of the profitability of an investment, calculated as the net gain or loss relative to the initial investment.

### STF- Security Token Offering
**Definition:** A fundraising method where security tokens representing ownership or equity in a company are sold to investors.

## Security Terms

### 2FA- Two-Factor Authentication
**Definition:** A security process that requires two forms of verification to access an account or perform transactions.

**AML- Anti-Money Laundering**
**Definition:** Regulations and procedures designed to prevent money laundering and financial crimes by verifying customer identities and monitoring transactions.

**DDoS- Distributed Denial of Service**
**Definition:** A cyber attack that overwhelms a network or website with excessive traffic, making it unavailable to users.

**DNS- Domain Name System**
**Definition:** A system that translates domain names (like www.example.com) into Internet Protocol (IP) addresses that computers use to identify each website on the network.

**SSL- Secure Sockets Layer**
**Definition:** A protocol for securing data transmitted over the internet by encrypting the connection between a web server and a browser.

Blockchain Terms

**DAO- Decentralized Autonomous Organization**
**Definition:** An organization represented by rules encoded in smart contracts on a blockchain, managed by its members through a voting system.

**GAS- Gas**
**Definition:** A unit of measurement used to quantify the computational effort required to perform transactions or execute smart contracts on the Ethereum network.

**Merkle Tree- Merkle Tree**
**Definition:** A data structure used to efficiently and securely verify the integrity of large sets of data, used in blockchain to ensure data consistency.

**Node- Node**
**Definition:** A computer that participates in a blockchain network, validating and relaying transactions and blocks.

## Miscellaneous Terms

**Satoshi- Satoshi**
**Definition:** The smallest unit of Bitcoin, named after its creator, Satoshi Nakamoto, equivalent to 0.00000001 BTC.

**Hashrate- Hashrate**
**Definition:** The measure of computational power used in mining or processing Cryptocurrency transactions, indicating how quickly hashes can be computed.

**Fork- Fork**
**Definition:** A change in the blockchain protocol that creates a divergence in the blockchain, resulting in a new version or a separate blockchain.

Understanding these abbreviations and their meanings can help you navigate the world of Cryptocurrency more effectively.

**Chapter-11: Some important "A to Z" simplified, point-by-point explanation of Cryptocurrency:**

**A**

- Address- A unique identifier in a blockchain network where Cryptocurrency can be sent or received, like a bank account number.
- Altcoin- Any Cryptocurrency other than Bitcoin (e.g., Ethereum, Litecoin).
- ASIC (Application-Specific Integrated Circuit)- Hardware designed specifically for mining Cryptocurrency.
- Airdrop- A method of distributing tokens for free, often to promote a project or reward early users.
- Atomic Swap- A smart contract technology that allows users to exchange one Cryptocurrency for another without using an intermediary, like an exchange.
- Automated Market Maker (AMM)- A type of decentralized exchange (DEX) protocol that uses liquidity pools instead of order books to facilitate trading.

**B**

- Blockchain- A decentralized digital ledger that records all transactions across a network of computers.

- Bitcoin- The first and most well-known Cryptocurrency, created by an anonymous person or group known as Satoshi Nakamoto.
- Block- A collection of transactions on the blockchain, which is confirmed and added to the chain.
- Burning- Permanently removing coins from circulation, reducing the total supply.
- Beacon Chain- The core chain in Ethereum 2.0 that coordinates shard chains and manages validators under the proof-of-stake consensus.
- Byzantine Fault Tolerance (BFT)- A property of blockchain systems that allows them to function properly even when some nodes act maliciously or are faulty.

## C

- Cryptography- The practice of securing information through codes, fundamental to ensuring the security and privacy of Cryptocurrency transactions.
- Coin- A Cryptocurrency that operates independently on its own blockchain (e.g., Bitcoin, Ethereum).
- Cold Wallet- An offline wallet used to store Cryptocurrency, considered more secure than online storage.
- Consensus Mechanism- The process by which blockchain participants agree on the state of the blockchain, ensuring everyone has the same version of the ledger. Some examples are Proof of Work (PoW), Proof of Stake (PoS), and Delegated Proof of Stake (DPoS).
- Custodial vs. Non-Custodial- Custodial wallets or services hold your private keys for you (like exchanges), whereas non-custodial wallets allow you to retain full control of your private keys.

# D

- Decentralized- No single entity (like a government or company) controls the Cryptocurrency network.
- DAO (Decentralized Autonomous Organization)- An organization run by smart contracts and decisions made by token holders rather than a central authority.
- DeFi (Decentralized Finance)- Financial services (like lending, borrowing) provided without traditional intermediaries, using blockchain technology.
- DAG (Directed Acyclic Graph)- An alternative data structure to blockchain, used by some cryptos (e.g., IOTA) to solve scalability issues by removing the concept of "blocks" entirely.
- dApp (Decentralized Application)- Applications that run on a decentralized network like Ethereum, without needing a central server or authority.
- Double Spend- A potential flaw in digital cash where the same token can be spent more than once. Blockchain prevents this by validating each transaction.

# E

- Ethereum- A blockchain that allows developers to build decentralized applications (dApps) and smart contracts, second most popular after Bitcoin.
- Exchange- A platform where users can buy, sell, and trade cryptocurrencies.
- EVM (Ethereum Virtual Machine)- The decentralized computer that runs smart contracts on the Ethereum network, capable of executing code in a trustless environment.
- Elliptic Curve Cryptography (ECC)- A cryptographic method used to create public-private key pairs, foundational in many blockchain platforms for securing data.

## F

- Fiat- Government-issued currency like the US dollar or Euro, used in contrast to Cryptocurrency.
- Fork- A split in a blockchain, creating two separate versions. Can be a -hard fork- (permanent) or -soft fork- (temporary).
- FOMO (Fear of Missing Out)- The psychological effect where investors buy into a Cryptocurrency because of fear that its price will skyrocket.
- Flash Loan- A type of uncollateralized loan available in DeFi, where users borrow and repay the loan within the same transaction. If they don't, the transaction is canceled.

## G

- Gas- A fee paid to execute transactions or run smart contracts on the Ethereum network.
- Genesis Block- The first block ever mined on a blockchain.
- Governance Token- A token that gives holders voting power in decentralized organizations, allowing them to influence protocol decisions and upgrades.
- Gas Limit- The maximum amount of gas (or computational power) a user is willing to spend on a transaction or smart contract execution.

## H

- Halving- An event where the reward for mining a block is reduced by half, usually occurring in Bitcoin every four years.
- Hash- A cryptographic function that takes an input and generates a fixed-size string of characters, which is used to secure blockchain transactions.
- HODL- A misspelled version of "hold," meaning to keep Cryptocurrency rather than selling it, even in volatile markets.
- Hash Rate- The computational power per second used by a Cryptocurrency network to validate transactions and add blocks. A higher hash rate means a more secure network.

- Hybrid PoW/PoS- A consensus mechanism combining Proof of Work (PoW) and Proof of Stake (PoS), allowing networks to benefit from both systems' advantages.

## I

- ICO (Initial Coin Offering)- A way for blockchain startups to raise funds by selling a new Cryptocurrency or token before it's publicly traded.
- Immutable- Data that cannot be changed once it's written on the blockchain.
- Interoperability- The ability of different blockchain networks to communicate and share information or tokens with each other, such as cross-chain swaps or bridges.
- IEO (Initial Exchange Offering)- A token sale conducted directly on a Cryptocurrency exchange platform, as opposed to an ICO.

## J

- JOMO (Joy of Missing Out)- In crypto, this refers to feeling happy about not participating in risky investments.
- JIT Liquidity (Just-In-Time Liquidity)- A strategy used by market participants in decentralized finance (DeFi) where liquidity is provided only when it is profitable, often used in automated market makers (AMMs).

## K

- KYC (Know Your Customer)- A process used by exchanges to verify the identity of their customers, typically to comply with legal regulations.
- Komodo- A multi-chain platform that provides security through its delayed Proof of Work (dPoW) consensus, allowing smaller chains to benefit from Bitcoin's security.
- Keypair- A set of a public and private key used in cryptography. Public keys are shared openly, while private keys are kept secret to control access to crypto assets.

# L

- Ledger- A record of all Cryptocurrency transactions, stored on the blockchain.
- Liquidity- The ease with which a Cryptocurrency can be bought or sold without affecting its price.
- Layer 1 vs. Layer 2- Layer 1 refers to the base blockchain architecture (e.g., Bitcoin, Ethereum), while Layer 2 refers to protocols built on top of Layer 1 to enhance scalability and speed (e.g., Lightning Network).
- Liquidity Mining- A way to earn tokens by providing liquidity to decentralized exchanges, usually by depositing tokens into liquidity pools.

# M

- Mining- The process of solving complex cryptographic puzzles to validate and add new transactions to a blockchain, earning new Cryptocurrency as a reward.
- Market Cap- The total value of all coins in circulation, calculated as (price per coin) x (number of coins).
- Merkle Tree- A structure used to efficiently and securely verify data integrity in a blockchain. Transactions are grouped in pairs, hashed, and the resulting hashes are hashed together until a single hash remains.
- Multi-Signature (Multisig)- A security feature requiring multiple private keys to authorize a Cryptocurrency transaction, often used in wallets or corporate environments for added security.

# N

- Node- A computer that connects to the blockchain network and helps validate and relay transactions.
- NFT (Non-Fungible Token)- A unique digital asset representing ownership of a specific item, like art or music, on a blockchain.

- Nonce- A random or unique number used once during the mining process to alter the hash of a block. Changing the nonce repeatedly helps miners find a valid hash that meets the blockchain's difficulty requirements.
- Nash Equilibrium- A concept from game theory applied in blockchain consensus mechanisms, where no participant has an incentive to deviate from the agreed-upon protocol because doing so would result in a worse outcome for them.

# O

- Oracles- Services that provide smart contracts with external data (e.g., weather, stock prices), necessary for executing certain conditions.
- Open Source- Software with publicly available code that anyone can inspect, modify, and enhance, often used in blockchain projects.
- Off-Chain vs. On-Chain- Off-chain refers to transactions or data handled outside the blockchain to reduce congestion and fees. On-chain refers to actions recorded directly on the blockchain, where they are visible and immutable.

# P

- Private Key- A secret key used to access and control your Cryptocurrency. If you lose it, you lose access to your funds.
- Public Key- The address you share with others to receive Cryptocurrency, derived from your private key.
- Plasma- A Layer 2 scaling solution for Ethereum, which uses "child" blockchains to offload transactions from the main chain, helping reduce congestion.
- Proof of Burn (PoB)- A consensus mechanism where miners "burn" coins (send them to an irretrievable address) in exchange for mining privileges.

## Q

- Quantum Computing- A potential future technology that could disrupt current cryptographic security by performing complex calculations at unimaginable speeds.
- Quorum- A blockchain platform developed by JPMorgan, designed for permissioned networks, offering enhanced privacy and performance features suitable for financial institutions.

## R

- ROI (Return on Investment)- A measure of how profitable an investment is, calculated as (gain from investment - cost of investment) / cost of investment.
- Rug Pull- A scam where developers abandon a project and run off with investors' money after raising funds.
- Rollups- A Layer 2 scaling solution for Ethereum, where transactions are "rolled up" and processed off-chain, with only a summary of the data submitted to the main chain. Optimistic Rollups and ZK-Rollups are common variants.
- Raiden Network- Ethereum's off-chain scaling solution similar to Bitcoin's Lightning Network, designed to enable faster and cheaper payments.

## S

- Smart Contract- A self-executing contract with the terms of the agreement written into code, which automatically enforces the contract's conditions.
- Stablecoin- A Cryptocurrency that's pegged to a stable asset like the US dollar, designed to minimize price volatility (e.g., Tether, USDC).
- Satoshi- The smallest unit of Bitcoin, equal to 0.00000001 BTC.
- Sharding- A technique that splits the blockchain into smaller, more manageable pieces called shards, each capable of processing its own transactions, increasing the network's capacity.

- Sidechain- A separate blockchain that is attached to the main chain and allows for interoperability between chains, often used for scaling or adding new features to a main blockchain.

# T

- Token- A type of Cryptocurrency built on an existing blockchain (e.g., ERC-20 tokens on Ethereum).
- TPS (Transactions Per Second)- A measure of how many transactions a blockchain can process per second.
- Turing Complete- A term used to describe a system that can perform any calculation given enough time and resources. Ethereum is considered Turing complete because its smart contracts can execute complex logic.
- Tokenomics- The study and design of a Cryptocurrency's economy, including its supply, demand, distribution, and incentives.

# U

- Utility Token- A token that gives users access to a product or service, rather than acting as a store of value like a coin.
- Unspent Transaction Output (UTXO)- The amount of Cryptocurrency remaining after a transaction that can be used as input for future transactions, commonly used in Bitcoin's system.
- Undercollateralization- A situation in DeFi where the value of the collateral provided for a loan is lower than the loan value, which introduces higher risks for lenders.

# V

- Validator- In proof-of-stake blockchains, validators are responsible for confirming transactions and adding them to the blockchain.
- Volatility- The degree of price fluctuation in the Cryptocurrency market.

- Validator Set- In PoS blockchains, the group of nodes responsible for validating new blocks and maintaining the network.
- Vanity Address- A public address that contains specific, recognizable patterns or words, often created for branding or fun.

## W

- Wallet- Software or hardware used to store and manage your Cryptocurrency keys (private and public).
- Whale- Someone who holds a large amount of Cryptocurrency and can significantly influence the market with their trades.
- Wrapped Tokens- Tokens that represent another Cryptocurrency on a different blockchain (e.g., Wrapped Bitcoin (WBTC) on Ethereum), allowing cross-chain compatibility.
- Whitelisting- In ICOs or token sales, the process of pre-approving participants to ensure they are allowed to buy tokens, often to comply with regulations.

## X

- XRP- The Cryptocurrency used by Ripple for fast, low-cost international payments.
- X-chain- Avalanche's decentralized platform allows for the creation and management of custom blockchain networks and assets across multiple chains, including its Exchange chain (X-chain).
- X-Dai- A stablecoin chain built on Ethereum but with much lower fees, designed for everyday transactions.

## Y

- Yield Farming- A way to earn rewards by lending or staking Cryptocurrency in decentralized finance (DeFi) platforms.
- Yield Aggregator- A DeFi tool that automates the process of finding and allocating funds to the most profitable yield

farming strategies, often dynamically moving funds across protocols to maximize returns.
- YAM Protocol- A DeFi project known for combining elastic supply mechanics (similar to Ampleforth) with governance tokens and yield farming.

# Z

- Zero-Knowledge Proof- A cryptographic method where one party proves to another that they know certain information without revealing the information itself.
- Zero-Knowledge Rollup (ZK-Rollup)- A Layer 2 scaling solution that uses zero-knowledge proofs to bundle many transactions together off-chain, while the rollup operator submits a validity proof back to the main chain, reducing the amount of data needed on-chain.
- ZK-SNARKs- A cryptographic method used in privacy-focused blockchains like Zcash, allowing transactions to be validated without revealing any information about the transaction details.

These important terms highlight the vast and complex world of Cryptocurrency beyond the basics, offering a deeper understanding of blockchain technology and its various components.

www.ingramcontent.com/pod-product-compliance
Lightning Source LLC
Chambersburg PA
CBHW050309230526
45471CB00005B/2098